Access to History
General Editor: Keith Randell

France and the Cardinals 1610-61

Richard Wilkinson

Hodder & Stoughton

A MEMBER OF THE HODDER HEADLINE GROUP

The cover illustration is a portrait of *Cardinal Richelieu* by Philippe de Champaigne (Courtesy of National Portrait Gallery, London).

Some other titles in the series:

Louis XIV, France and Europe 1661-1715 ISBN 0 340 57511 5
Richard Wilkinson

France: Renaissance, Religion and Recovery 1483-1610 ISBN 0 340 51804 9
Martyn Rady

Spain: Rise and Decline 1474-1643 ISBN 0 340 51807 3
Jill Kilsby

Sweden and the Baltic 1523-1721 ISBN 0 340 54644 1
Andrina Stiles

The Ottoman Empire 1450-1700 ISBN 0 340 56999 9
Andrina Stiles

British Library Cataloguing in Publication Data

A catalogue for this is available
from the British Library

ISBN 0-340-61115-4

First published 1995

Impression number	10 9 8 7 6 5 4 3 2 1
Year	1999 1998 1997 1996 1995

Typeset by Sempringham publishing services, Bedford
Printed in Great Britain for Hodder & Stoughton Educational,
a division of Hodder Headline Plc, 338 Euston Road, London NW1 3BH
by Redwood Books, Trowbridge, Wiltshire

Contents

Author's Acknowledgements

The following have helped me with this short book. My wife has read the proofs, repeatedly corrected my spelling and made constructive comments. Robin Briggs has generously given me of his time and erudition. Philip Lough has made available his knowledge of colloquial seventeenth century French. Keith Randell has provided me with editorial encouragement and advice. David Lea and Clare Weaver of Hodder and Stoughton have been supportive. Peter Ford and my other Marlborough colleagues have provided a stimulating environment in which to teach, think and write. However none of these people should be blamed for the book's defects which are my own.

Dedication

For the History Department at Marlborough College

Preface

To the general reader

Although the *Access to History* series has been designed with the needs of students studying the subject at higher examination levels very much in mind, it also has a great deal to offer the general reader. The main body of the text (i.e. ignoring the Study Guides at the ends of chapters) forms a readable and yet stimulating survey of a coherent topic as studied by historians. However, each author's aim has not merely been to provide a clear explanation of what happened in the past (to interest and inform): it has also been assumed that most readers wish to be stimulated into thinking further about the topic and to form opinions of their own about the significance of the events that are described and discussed (to be challenged). Thus, although no prior knowledge of the topic is expected on the reader's part, she or he is treated as an intelligent and thinking person throughout. The author tends to share ideas and possibilities with the reader, rather than passing on numbers of so-called 'historical truths'.

To the student reader

There are many ways in which the series can be used by students studying History at a higher level. It will, therefore, be worthwhile thinking about your own study strategy before you start your work on this book. Obviously, your strategy will vary depending on the aim you have in mind, and the time for study that is available to you.

If, for example, you want to acquire a general overview of the topic in the shortest possible time, the following approach will probably be the most effective:

1 Read chapter 1 and think about its contents.
2 Read the 'Making notes' section at the end of chapter 2 and decide whether it is necessary for you to read this chapter.
3 If it is, read the chapter, stopping at each heading to note down the main points that have been made.
4 Repeat stage 2 (and stage 3 where appropriate) for all the other chapters.

If, however, your aim is to gain a thorough grasp of the topic, taking however much time is necessary to do so, you may benefit from carrying out the same procedure with each chapter, as follows:

1 Read the chapter as fast as you can, and preferably at one sitting.
2 Study the flow diagram at the end of the chapter, ensuring that you understand the general 'shape' of what you have just read.

3 Read the 'Making notes' section (and the 'Answering essay questions' section, if there is one) and decide what further work you need to do on the chapter. In particularly important sections of the book, this will involve reading the chapter a second time and stopping at each heading to think about (and to write a summary of) what you have just read.
4 Attempt the 'Source-based questions' section. It will sometimes be sufficient to think through your answers, but additional understanding will often be gained by forcing yourself to write them down.

When you have finished the main chapters of the book, study the 'Further Reading' section and decide what additional reading (if any) you will do on the topic.

This book has been designed to help make your studies both enjoyable and successful. If you can think of ways in which this could have been done more effectively, please write to tell me. In the meantime, I hope that you will gain greatly from your study of History.

Keith Randell

Acknowledgements

The Publishers would like to thank the following for permission to reproduce illustrations in this volume:

Cover - Cardinal Richelieu by Philippe de Champaigne, The National Portrait Gallery, London.

Agnew and Sons, London / The Bridgeman Art Library p. 5; Prado, Madrid / The Bridgeman Art Library p. 6; Giraudon / The Bridgeman Art Library p. 35; Musée Condé / The Bridgeman Art Library p. 87.

Every effort has been made to trace and acknowledge ownership of copyright. The Publishers will be glad to make suitable arrangements with any copyright holders whom it has not been possible to contact.

CHAPTER 1

Introduction: The Case for Absolutism

1 Interpretations and Controversies

How do governments work? How do they get people to comply with their instructions, especially when on the face of it those instructions are absurd or misconceived? Why does anyone pay taxes, obey laws and even suffer or die for a government? These are rightly the concerns of historians, for the pursuit of such questions takes us to the very heart of a civilisation. Consider a stone-age monument like Silbury Hill in north Wiltshire. What an extraordinary way of life it must represent! Is it the product of religion or tyranny, or both? Or take Norman England. 'The Normans were great castle-builders', the text-books tell us. 'No they were not', we should reply, for those castles were built by English peasants - in order to guarantee their own subjection to an alien Norman baron. Here we can indeed identify a society based on coercion. In our 'civilized' times we co-operate because of our so-called democratic consensus - or as some would argue, because we are conned by the government of the day. The fact is that down the ages rulers have operated in the context of their own social and political environment, exacting obedience either through terror, bribery or bamboozlement. The mixture has varied according to the subtlety and sophistication of the available means of persuasion.

This book explores politics and society in France between 1610 and 1661. It investigates how centralised royal government actually worked during this period. It is a fascinating and indeed puzzling case-study. Anyone who has motored through France must be impressed by its size. Four hundred years ago it was an even bigger place from the point of view of the government in Paris. There were no telephones, no railways, and not even any properly surfaced roads to enable instructions to be quickly conveyed and enforced. About eighteen million French people confronted the king, his handful of administrators and a royal army which was often quite small and therefore capable of dominating only a limited part of the country at any one time. Aristocrats backed by hordes of private retainers could snap their fingers at the distant monarch, while peasants could ignore government edicts with their traditional mulish obstinacy. The countryside was infested with gangs of highwaymen and escaped criminals. Yet it seems that governments succeeded in governing. It appears that the French generally complied with instructions emanating from Paris. And what is so astonishing is the extent to which they suffered, died, and above all paid for the policies adopted by their political masters. It is a strange story. How was such an apparently remarkable exercise in governmental control accomplished?

For many years historians were agreed on the right answer to this question. They argued that France was governed so effectively because of royal absolutism, methodically and ruthlessly established by two great ministers, Cardinal Richelieu and Cardinal Mazarin. Absolutism means government unrestrained by constitutional checks such as responsibility to parliament, the rights of subjects, and the supremacy of law; it anticipates totalitarianism, the twentieth century version of absolutism. Richelieu imposed absolutism from 1624 until his death in 1642 on behalf of his royal master Louis XIII. Mazarin continued Richelieu's work in the name of the boy-king Louis XIV from 1643 until his own death in 1661.

The analysis presented by this 'old' orthodoxy can be summarised as follows. Royal absolutism flourished in seventeenth-century France to a great extent because of the subservience of Frenchmen to their monarchs. It was a conformist, class-ridden society. The Catholic church combined with art and literature to persuade the French to obey their kings. All that was needed was a self-confident and efficient monarch. However, for one reason or another, the kings from 1610 to 1661 were not up to the job. After the assassination in 1610 of the first Bourbon ruler, the strong and effective Henri IV, the political credibility of the French royal family was consistently weak. The regency of the foolish queen-mother, Marie de Medici, paved the way for the ineffectual rule of the unbalanced Louis XIII. His early death led to another regency by another queen-mother, Anne of Austria, on behalf of her son, Louis XIV. The cardinals compensated for these inadequate figureheads by acting as chief ministers on their behalf. Richelieu and Mazarin, backed up by their teams of sinister *intendants* (trouble-shooters or busy-bodies, according to your point of view) created the absolutist state - an achievement certainly beyond the feeble powers of France's theoretical 'rulers'. By their ruthlessness the cardinals saved France from anarchy at home. By their calculated, aggressive foreign policy they saved France from humiliation abroad.

This interpretation has recently been questioned. It has been pointed out - by Roger Mettam, for example - that 'absolutism' was not a seventeenth-century word and that the whole concept is an over-simplification of a complex story. Mettam has argued that the power of seventeenth-century French governments was severely limited - not only by distance, the sheer numbers of people to be ruled and the lack of the coercive methods of punishment which twentieth century tyrants have at their disposal, but above all by entrenched privileges, interest-groups and corruption. His claim is that if Richelieu and Mazarin did achieve anything, it was by compromise, judicious concessions and tactical alliances with aristocratic power-élites.

It is argued that 'patronage', 'faction' and 'local interest groups' are more fruitful topics for investigation and research than 'absolutism'. The role of the *intendant* for instance has been reassessed against the background of local politics. The conclusion has been that, although seventeenth-century France may well have been a king-worshipping society, it was also an age in which other loyalties operated - to one's family, to one's locality, and to one's professional organisation. The contributions of 'great men' are seen as less significant than the wheelings and dealings involving local magnates, office-holders and urban élites. Furthermore, this 'structuralist' approach, stressing the importance of impersonal elements in French society, questions the significance of the cardinals' 'absolutist' policies, for it emphasises continuity as opposed to change. It claims that such key factors as the use of *intendants,* the sale and exploitation of office, and the role of the aristocracy in local government can be traced back into the sixteenth century. It is maintained in a similar way that such trends were to develop and evolve long after Richelieu's and Louis XIV's alleged revolutions in government.

Where the contributions of the so-called great men have been admitted, they too have been reassessed. Their weaknesses and failures, as well as their successes, have been emphasised. Not even Henri IV has been immune from criticism. The ephemeral fragility of his achievements has been pin-pointed, for it is now perceived how little had been settled both at home and abroad when he met his end. Both Richelieu and Mazarin are now portrayed as fallible and vulnerable politicians, opportunists and gamblers whose projects often blew up in their faces. Their achievements were flawed and partial. Conversely Louis XIII is now seen in a more favourable light. He was the master, Richelieu his servant. It is said that Mazarin depended from first to last on Anne of Austria's support, while even Marie de Medici has her defenders.

While this 'revisionism', that is to say the challenging of previously accepted orthodoxy, is no doubt salutary, it has not been totally accepted. Maybe the cardinals were not quite as infallible as their admirers have maintained. But perhaps what is needed is a re-interpretation of their methods rather than a denial of their achievements. 'Absolutism' may not be a seventeenth-century term, yet Frenchmen certainly spoke and wrote of 'absolute kingship'. Indeed one recent historian, David Parker, entitled his book *The Making of French Absolutism* (published in 1983). Whatever one wants to call it, royal government achieved much, especially in the context of tax-collecting. However unedifying, the extraction of millions of livres out of the French population during the reigns of Louis XIII and Louis XIV was a major feat, for no-one likes paying tax, especially if he is near to destitution and starvation. Not even the revisionists can deny this achievement. Any discussion of French government and society must take it into account - and this is only one, though perhaps the most spectacular, of the triumphs of French 'absolutism'.

In this book an attempt will be made to do justice to the two main schools of interpretation outlined above, while readers will be encouraged to make up their own minds about their relative merits. However, the term 'absolutism' will certainly be used, as this seems to be appropriate provided one is aware of the practical limitations under which royal government operated. At least it is less clumsy than alternatives such as 'authoritarian royal government acting within severely circumscribed parameters'!

Of course, whether we can meaningfully speak of 'absolutism' is clearly not the most interesting and important question. Far more rewarding areas of study are the methods and achievements of seventeenth-century French governments. These must be set against their social and political background. What sort of a society did the cardinals attempt to govern? What were the popular reactions to their policies and achievements? What part did religion play in influencing the policies of these princes of the church and in the reactions of a mainly Catholic nation? Above all, were the policies chosen by Richelieu and Mazarin necessarily the right ones? Were the long-term interests of the French people best served by the cardinals' implementation of absolutism? Indeed, were there viable alternatives?

2 The Years of Drift, 1610-24

The period 1610-24 forms an interlude between the authoritarian regimes of Henri IV and Cardinal Richelieu. Traditionally historians have regarded these years as fundamentally sterile, as a time of drift, fully justifying the stern measures adopted by Richelieu who re-established the authority of the crown and restored coherence and a sense of purpose to government policy. Is this an accurate assessment?

a) The Regency of Marie de Medici

On 14 May 1610 Henri IV was at the height of his power. Otherwise known as Henri of Navarre, the first Bourbon king was a bandy-legged little man with a bulbous nose. Even by the standards of an unhygienic age he stank. All his many mistresses were bought - they had to be. However, while he may have had his failings, 'Henri the Great', as court flatterers called him, was admired and respected, for in truth he had much to his credit. He had brought peace and orderly government to a realm distracted by religious and factional wars. The crown was now making a profit. The succession was guaranteed by two legitimate sons. Self-confident, forceful, actively involved in government, Henri IV was the most effective ruler France had had for half a century.

Yet the king was busy making a fool of himself over a fifteen-year-old girl. Though arguably he should have known better at his age (he was fifty-seven), Henri had fallen for Charlotte de Montmorency. He ingeniously arranged her marriage to his cousin Condé who was reputedly homosexual and therefore unlikely to object to an affair between his wife and the king. But that was not how it turned out. Condé played the jealous husband and decamped with his wife to Brussels, in the Spanish Netherlands. The Habsburg regent refused to hand over the couple. For the love-sick king of France that meant war.

As it happened this fitted in well with Henri IV's foreign policy. Traditionally, French kings opposed the ambitions of the Habsburgs whose territories encircled France; to the south was Spain, to the north were the Spanish Netherlands, and to the east lay Germany whose princes owed allegiance to the Habsburg emperor with his Austrian power-base. Recently Henri's diplomacy had supported German princes who opposed the emperor over the succession to the strategically vital Rhineland duchies of Julich and Cleves (see the map on page 123). Charlotte's flit to Brussels was just the provocation that Henri needed to translate words into deeds; Habsburg pride must be humbled.

The Catholic king of France did not care that his German allies were Protestant. In the words of a recent historian, Henri 'was too flippant to be a fanatic'. But it did worry his more devout Catholic subjects. And it was an unbalanced Catholic schoolmaster, François de Ravaillac, who climbed into the royal carriage and stabbed Henri in the heart. Ravaillac was subsequently covered with molten lead and soaked in boiling oil

Louis XIII by Frans Pourbus the Younger

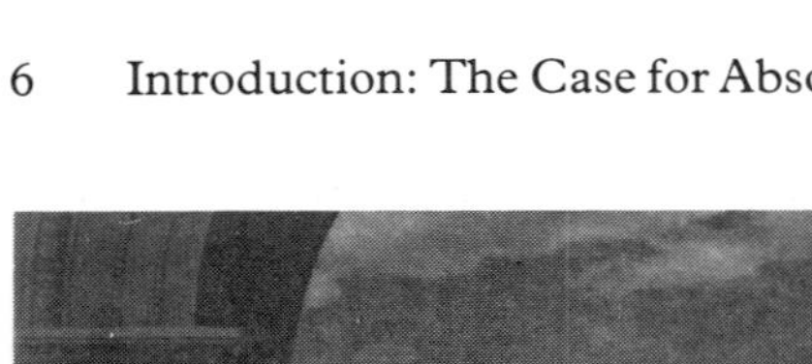

Marie de Medici by Frans Pourbus the Younger, 1617

before being torn to pieces by four wild horses; but throughout these atrocious ordeals he denied that he had accomplices, he just wanted to prevent France siding with heretics against the Catholic Habsburgs. It was ironic that the most tolerant of kings should perish at the hand of a religious crackpot.

The news of the murder caused panic in Paris. Whatever people thought of Henri's foreign policy, there was no mistaking the threat of renewed violence and instability caused by his death. 'The king is dead!' blubbered his widow, Marie de Medici. 'No, Madam', replied the Chancellor, 'the king is standing next to you' - and he indicated the gauche, sullen eight-year-old who stared in bewilderment at the weeping adults. It was indeed an inauspicious beginning for Louis XIII's reign. While technically the Chancellor was right, the tears of the Queen Mother were only too realistic. For the next half-century the leaders of French society tore each other apart in their attempts to come to terms with the consequences of Henri's murder.

The basic issue was this: could the crown recover the self-confident effectiveness of Henri IV's day, or would the many disruptive forces in French society succeed in destroying the fragile social and political stability which Henri had established? This is the theme of this book. Certainly the situation was brutally clarified during the years immediately following Henri IV's murder.

From 1610 to 1617 Marie de Medici ruled France as regent on behalf of her son. This Italian princess enjoyed power, though whether she used it wisely has been questioned. To be fair, she has not had a generous press. The regent's French contemporaries blamed her - a little harshly - for being a woman, a foreigner and a *parvenue*. Rubens' portrait of 'the banker's daughter' - as the French cruelly nicknamed her - makes her look fat and bovine, 'like a gorgeously bedizened barmaid', as one historian has put it. Marie handled her children badly. She was excessively influenced by her Italian favourites. After Louis XIII expressed his thanks for her efforts by expelling her from court, Marie displayed an unattractive mixture of resentment, treachery and stupidity. On the other hand, she had maintained the authority of the crown in exceptionally difficult circumstances. On the whole she had avoided war. She had spotted Richelieu's ability. Years before Henri IV had summed up the regency of Marie's relative Catherine de Medici: 'I am astonished that she did not do worse'. Maybe a similar verdict could be passed on Marie.

Her first measures were sensible. In 1611 she concluded peace with the Habsburgs, after French troops had captured Julich. An era of European peace was made possible in 1615 by the double marriages of Louis XIII to the king of Spain's daughter Anne, and of Louis' sister Elizabeth to the heir to the Spanish throne, the future Philip IV. Marie retained the ablest of her husband's ministers - Villeroy (foreign affairs), Jeannin (finance) and Sillery (the chancellor). However, after a few months she discarded the overbearing and unpopular Sully. His rigid economies had created a substantial cash reserve which Marie wished to spend; Sully would certainly disapprove, so he had to go. Marie spent money on palace decorations and entertainments, appreciating the propaganda value of a more splendid court than the informal shambles maintained by her rough-and-ready husband. And she tried to retain the loyalty and co-operation of the influential nobles who were excluded from government by bribing them (4,000,000 livres to Condé, 1,300,000 livres to Conti, 1,200,000 livres to Nevers). Given their greed and lust for power, this was an understandable policy.

Unfortunately it did not work. In the spring of 1614 the regent was confronted with a major revolt, which set the pattern for future acts of defiance of royal authority. First, princes of the blood (the king's relations) were involved, notably the ambitious and unreliable Condé and Vendôme, one of Henri IV's many bastards. Secondly, there was a dangerous religious element. France contained a sizeable Protestant minority known as the Huguenots. They had been awarded liberty of worship and military guarantees by the Edict of Nantes (1598). However, the Huguenots were aware of their unpopularity with the Catholic majority of French people and were apprehensive about such developments as the Queen Mother's pro-Catholic foreign policy. The leading Huguenot nobleman, Bouillon, therefore added his own private army to Condé's troops. Overmighty magnates could always create trouble in the remoter parts of France where their authority was liable to be greater than the crown's. So now Condé raised the standard of revolt in Normandy and Bouillon in Provence.

Marie defeated the revolt with a combination of energy, concessions and luck. She took the king with her on a royal progress through the Loire valley, then to Angers, Nantes and Chartres. It was good tactics to parade royal authority in key areas which otherwise might have joined the rebels. Further bribes and well-paid jobs were judiciously distributed. A more radical concession was Marie's agreement to the nobles' demand that the Estates General should be summoned - a development to which we shall turn shortly. She was lucky in two respects. First, the leaders of the revolt were ineffectual and unpopular, utterly failing to attract widespread support. Secondly, the 1614 episode was not typical of past and future revolts in that there was no foreign involvement. Spain was friendly, the emperor was distracted, James I of England interfered but was so ineffectual that he could be ignored. A European power vacuum favoured the regent's chances of re-establishing royal authority.

But she had promised to summon the Estates General. This was a significant concession, for traditionally the Estates only met when the crown was weak. The procedure was that representatives of the three Estates - clergy, nobility and the rest - met together in order to present their *cahiers des doléances* (summaries of grievances) of which the king was obliged to take note. Significantly the Estates met in 1560, 1576, 1588 and illegally in 1593, that is to say during the chaos and instability of the wars of religion. After the Estates met in 1614-15, they were not to meet again until 1789 - the event which triggered the French Revolution.

If the disaffected nobles hoped to exploit the meeting of the Estates General to bolster their own positions and humiliate the regent, they failed. Marie de Medici outmanoeuvred her enemies. First she exerted the crown's influence over the election of deputies. On the whole she succeeded in procuring the return of men who were loyal to the crown rather than to Condé or Bouillon. These included a significant number of royal officials. Furthermore Marie ensured that the spokesmen for each of the Estates could be relied on to exercise a moderating influence. Lastly, when the debates got underway her interventions were occasional but effective.

Not that there was any danger of a united opposition emerging. The three Estates were soon quarrelling with each other. Reforming bishops, on behalf of the First Estate, demanded the introduction and implementation of the decrees of the Council of Trent which had launched the Counter-Reformation. Not only was this demand opposed by the Third Estate, always suspicious of ecclesiastical influence, but it was even disputed by other members of the First Estate, especially cathedral canons who were opposed to interference by the papacy in the affairs of the French church. The Second Estate demanded the abolition of the sale of offices by which the lawyers of the Third Estate got rich, and the Third Estate wanted an end to the nobility's pensions. As for the impertinent suggestion by one of the Third Estate's deputies that the nobles were 'our brothers', this brought the stinging retort: 'We do not want the children of shoemakers and cobblers to call us brothers'. One of the most interesting debates concerned the clergy's defence of tyrannicide if the king were a heretic. This was in response to the Third Estate's condemnation of the murder of kings in any circumstances. Marie tactfully intervened to state that the Third Estate's views were noted but would not be accepted in the official summary of grievances.

Arguments and quarrels continued throughout the winter of 1614-15. There was certainly widespread dissatisfaction with the government's extravagance, high taxation and inefficiency. Reforms were clearly necessary, but there was no agreement about which reforms should be introduced and how they were to be implemented. Marie was increasingly irked by such criticisms. She agreed to the temporary abolition of the *paulette* (the system whereby official positions could be passed on to relatives in return for an annual cash payment to the crown), but made no other concessions. Eventually she commanded considerable support when she maintained that the Estates were futile and time-wasting, in no way justifying the expenditure of public money. The final ceremony occurred on 23 February 1615 in the presence of the regent. The three Estates made their last pleas for reforms: laws were to be simplified, taxes were to be reduced, and corrupt middlemen were to be removed. It was even suggested that curés (parish priests) should be elected by their parishioners. The spokesman for the Third Estate delivered his speech on his knees. Even more obsequious was the spokesman for the First Estate, who praised the Queen-Mother's wise rule, in particular the Spanish marriages and her harshness towards the Huguenots; he was the 29-year-old bishop of Luçon, an ambitious aristocrat named Armand-Jean du Plessis de Richelieu of whom we shall hear again.

What an instructive comparison between the Estates General and the contemporary English parliament! Due no doubt to France's more rigid class structure, how little understanding or fellow-feeling there was between the three Estates! The contrast with the basic sympathy between the English Lords and Commons, many of whose members were related, could not be greater. The subservience of the Third Estate to the other two is as striking as the complete absence in England of a vocal and organised political wing of the church. Whereas English monarchs since Henry VIII had, with varying degrees of enthusiasm, involved parliament in legislation and decision-making, the Estates General had only met intermittently, with no clear purpose or rôle. This showed both in the total absence of leadership and in the internecine bickering. When an intrepid deputy suggested that the Estates should not be dismissed until grievances were answered, the regent angrily retorted that there were to be no innovations. Soon afterwards the deputies meekly dispersed with little achieved.

However, Marie de Medici was sufficiently impressed by the bishop of Luçon to make him her chaplain and before long a member of her government. She now felt confident enough to dismiss the 'greybeards', as her husband's ministers were called, and introduce new men such as Richelieu whom she made secretary for military and foreign affairs. More provocative was the favour shown to her Italian foster-sister, the midget Leonora Galligai, who was believed to exercise supernatural influence over the gullible regent, and Leonora's greedy and arrogant husband, Concino Concini. This unattractive pair shamelessly enriched themselves and their relations. Concini promoted himself Marshal of France and marquis d'Ancre, while Leonora's brother became Archbishop of Tours. Everybody crawled to them, especially Richelieu who adopted Concini as his patron. But Marie's supreme blunder was to ignore and alienate her own son, the king. 'Run away and play', she told the shy adolescent when he timidly sidled into the council chamber. Others had the sense to pay him more attention. For both perceptive courtiers and ruthless adventurers realised that the future lay with Louis XIII.

In April 1617 a plot was hatched between Condé and Luynes, the king's falconer, to murder Concini and banish the Queen Mother. Louis was an enthusiastic participator and waited on tenterhooks for news that all was well. It was a botched and bloody business, but Concini was eventually shot, his guards disarmed and Marie de Medici bundled off to imprisonment at Blois. Courtiers and politicians hastened to establish their credentials with the new regime. Some succeeded, but not Richelieu. That self-propelling bishop was dismissed by his monarch, who was triumphantly standing on a billiard-table: 'Now at last, Luçon, I am free of your tyranny. Be off with you, get out of here!'. Richelieu hastily obeyed. On the way back to his lodgings his carriage got wedged in a mob tearing Concini's corpse to pieces. Richelieu did not intervene on behalf of his late-patron's remains, and was glad to avoid his fate. Leonora Galligai was less fortunate. After she had been condemned as a witch by the Parlement of Paris, she was beheaded and her corpse was burnt.

b) The King theoretically in Control, 1617-24

Any purposeful direction of government which Marie had achieved now disappeared. In theory Louis XIII was in charge, with Luynes as chief minister. But this amiable, middle-aged bumbler had almost certainly reached his ceiling as keeper of the king's falcons. The government now lurched from crisis to crisis. Whereas Marie had given France peace, Louis XIII and Luynes initiated an expensive and damaging civil war. Louis was much influenced by the Catholic reformers who were beginning to exert effective control on the education of aristocratic Frenchmen. The existence of the embattled Huguenot minority in the heart of his realm was therefore an offence to the king. The Huguenots had on occasions put themselves in the wrong by flirting with trouble-makers such as Condé. But the majority were loyal to the crown, anxious not to give offence. Nevertheless the Most Christian King, as the French monarch was traditionally called, was determined to persecute these potentially dangerous though temporally quiescent Protestants.

The occasion for attacking his own subjects was offered to Louis XIII by Marie de Medici. The redoubtable Queen Mother escaped from the castle in which she was confined by climbing down a rope. Due to her weight the rope snapped, depositing her in the moat. Passing soldiers jeered at her, mistaking her for a whore. But she still succeeded in instigating a rebellion. Louis raised troops who easily dispersed the rebels. He then turned his army south and attacked the Huguenots of Béarn, adjacent to the recently incorporated kingdom of Navarre. Without difficulty he defeated the Huguenots and re-established Catholic worship. But Louis had stirred up a hornets' nest. Huguenots throughout France were by now thoroughly alarmed for their own safety. Led by the duc de Rohan they erupted in revolt. Throughout 1621 and 1622 Louis led his armies against Huguenot rebels. Victory in the field proved relatively easy - for Louis was a rather good strategist. But the capture of Huguenot strongholds was lengthy, tedious and dangerous. In 1621 the siege of Montauban was abandoned after heavy losses, including Luynes who died of camp fever. Montpellier defied Louis XIII in 1622, until both sides agreed to a compromise peace: many Huguenot fortresses were to be razed but not the most important, Montpellier and La Rochelle. These terms upset the Huguenots who regrouped their forces for the next round, while the *dévots,* as the more enthusiastic Catholics were called, were furious that the heretics had been treated so leniently; it was all most unsatisfactory - clearly from every point of view a case of unfinished business.

This futile and unsatisfactory civil war was a distraction from momentous developments in Europe to which the French government should have given its undivided attention. In 1618 the Thirty Years War broke out - a gruesome, titanic struggle which was to devastate Germany and involve all the continental powers. Habsburg domination of Europe was ultimately prevented. But the cost was immense, partly because of a series of preventable Habsburg triumphs between 1618 and 1621 - triumphs which Louis XIII's government actually assisted, due to his enthusiastic Catholicism. For instance, Louis XIII persuaded the German princes to remain neutral while the leading Protestant, Frederick the Elector Palatine of the Rhine, was defeated in his attempt to retain the throne of Bohemia. These developments were clearly detrimental to French security, which was threatened by Habsburg ambitions.

Indeed a powerful clique of patriotic Frenchmen, known as the *bons Français,* demanded measures to check Habsburg imperialism. They pointed out the sinister Latin message contained in the vowels A-E-I-O-U: Austriae Est Imperare Orbi Universae (it is Austria's destiny to rule the whole earth). Something must be done. Due to this pressure from the *bons Français* Louis agreed to his sister Henrietta Maria's marriage to the Protestant Charles, Prince of Wales, soon to become Charles I of England. Louis' government also exerted diplomatic pressure on behalf of the Protestant Grissons who controlled the strategically vital Valtelline pass (see the map on page 123). However, the Spaniards succeeded in gaining control of the area, which enabled them to dispatch troops from their recruiting ground in northern Italy to Germany and the Netherlands. For all his Catholic enthusiasm, Louis XIII resented this humiliation intensely.

The minister responsible for foreign policy, La Vieuville, personified the inadequacy of Louis XIII's government. He was outmanoeuvred by the Spanish in the Valtelline affair which infuriated the *bons Français.* He bungled Henrietta Maria's marriage negotiations, failing to extract from the English government satisfactory guarantees for Catholics in England, which infuriated the *dévots.* He combined personal enrichment with public economies, which made him many enemies. He was attacked by a virulent series of pamphlets, inspired by Richelieu who coveted his job. There was concern at the government's lack of direction and increasing unanimity that Richelieu should be recruited. Unfortunately Louis could not stand him. Maybe he associated Richelieu with the Queen Mother. Maybe he liked robust, virile men around him to compensate for his own ill-health - and Richelieu was a frail invalid. Meanwhile La Vieuville lurched from crisis to crisis.

The king's reluctance to change his ministers was finally overcome by an alliance which testified to Richelieu's manipulative skills. His most powerful advocate was Marie de Medici. In 1621 Richelieu had negotiated a temporary reconciliation between Marie and the king, as a result of which she returned to the council. Marie repaid Richelieu by persuading her son to support Richelieu's campaign for a cardinal's hat which was successfully concluded in 1622. Curiously Richelieu was supported both by the *dévots* and the *bons Français;* both parties believed that he shared their aspirations and would put them into effect. Finally, the case for taking Richelieu on board was supported by the unfortunate La Vieuville who was soon to be dispatched to a dungeon. Faced by this impressive array of the cardinal's admirers Louis XIII reluctantly gave way. In April 1624 Richelieu was admitted to the Council, in August he became chief minister. For better or for worse, the years of drift were over.

So what are the lessons of these seemingly aimless fourteen years? Contemporaries and historians are agreed that they demonstrated some disturbing facts of life. First, the reality of the Habsburg threat to the European balance of power and therefore to French security was now uncomfortably apparent. Secondly, the forces which had disrupted France during the latter part of the sixteenth century were still unpleasantly virile. Thirdly, and arising logically from the first two facts of life, was the self-evident need for firm government.

But where was this firm government to be found? Could this come from any other source except the king or his ministers? Was there any chance, for instance, that some form of quasi-representative government would emerge as had occurred in Holland and would eventually happen in England? Sadly the message of the meeting of the Estates General in 1614-15 was the three estates' total inability to co-operate with each other, to agree on a programme of reform, or to instigate an alternative system of government. Even if some of their reforms were quite sensible, there was no practical way in which they could impose them on a reluctant crown. Or could the nobles establish an oligarchy as an alternative to monarchy? Probably not, for time and again during these fourteen years they had demonstrated their selfish irresponsibilty and total unsuitability for national leadership.

But if the only realistic hope of stability and firm, consistent policy-making rested with the crown, it was unfortunately clear that the Queen Mother and her son, Louis XIII, were unable to provide what was required. Both seemed incapable of pursuing coherent policies themselves or of selecting ministers who were up to the job. The king in particular was a complex bundle of inhibitions. He was not a fool, and a recent biographer, A. Lloyd Moote, has argued that between 1617 and 1624 he established the basic priorities which Richelieu was to follow. But Louis was disastrously lacking in self-confidence - he was morbidly aware of his widely-perceived inferiority to his popular predecessor. 'Do I stink like my father?' he asked hopefully. In retrospect there seems to have been only one answer: a chief minister who would govern the country on the king's behalf, recruiting an effective team of like-minded administrators. Richelieu was waiting. All that was needed was Louis XIII's readiness to accept this unattractive but increasingly unavoidable option. Richelieu liked to convey the impression that his rise to power was inevitable. As we shall see in chapter 3, recent research has demonstrated that it was no such thing. Nevertheless if there had indeed to be a strong lead from the centre, was there any alternative to Richelieu and his version of royal absolutism?

Perhaps there was not. Certainly the events of 1610-24 made both absolutism and Richelieu attractive options. But we should always beware of saying that there were no alternatives and at this stage of our explorations we should keep open minds. We shall see that as things turned out Richelieu's domestic and foreign policies, in other words his implementations of absolutism, were to inflict on the French people untold miseries - miseries only to be surpassed by Louis XIV's absolutism. Did this really have to happen? This is a complex question. In order to begin to answer it we need to investigate French government and society more thoroughly - our task in the next chapter.

Making notes on *'Introduction - The Case for Absolutism'*

Absolutism is a recurrent theme in this book and in historians' discussions of the period 1610 to 1661 (and beyond). You should therefore begin a businesslike note headed 'Absolutism', leaving plenty of space for later entries as the story develops. At this stage use the material from the first part of this chapter in order to establish on paper and in your mind a clear definition of absolutism in general (i.e. as a philosophical concept) and of absolutism in the context of seventeenth century France. Then summarise the controversy between the traditional orthodoxy, which accepts absolutism as a valid description of theory and practice in the period studied in this book, and recent revisionism which questions the usefulness of the term. What is the difference between 'absolutism' and 'totalitarianism'?

Next make a careful note on the alleged case for absolutism due to the aimlessness of royal government between 1610 and 1624. This will involve you in an assessment of Marie de Medici - 'for and against'. Make a separate note on the Estates General of 1614-1615, a very significant episode. Summarise the characteristics of Louis XIII's attempts at personal rule between 1617 and 1624. Link these developments with the appointment of Richelieu as chief minister.

***Answering essay questions on** 'Introduction - The Case for Absolutism'*

Examiners rarely ask questions specifically on the period 1610-1624. On the other hand, the material in this first chapter is highly relevant to questions on absolutism during the ministries of Richelieu and Mazarin. Nor can questions requiring an assessment of Richelieu's problems, policies and achievements be answered satisfactorily without knowledge of the political background.

CHAPTER 2

The State of a Nation

The purpose of this chapter is to establish the context in which the cardinals governed France on behalf of their royal masters. What sort of a country was France between 1610 and 1661? This might seem a relatively straightforward question, devoid of controversy. Even so, truly to enter the world of Richelieu and Mazarin makes demands on our imagination and understanding. Empathy cannot easily be acquired with the inhabitants of such an unfamiliar landscape.

Having analysed the general environment in which the cardinals operated, we shall examine the social and political dynamics of the land which they governed. What chance had France's rulers of ruling effectively and of implementing the objectives of so-called absolutism? Indeed, could the cardinals attempt to achieve anything of the sort? What realistic options were actually available? Have we a story of change or of continuity? Here we definitely enter the realms of controversy. Our approach at this stage must be to attempt to understand the findings of recent scholarship as we explore the nature and sources of political power, both at the centre and in France's localities. When readers reach the end of this book they will have to decide whether the latest interpretations are valid or whether revisionism has gone too far.

The chapter concludes with the strange couple who in theory - and some historians now say in practice - exercised reponsibility for the welfare and security of eighteen million French people.

1 Early Modern - or Late Medieval?

We begin with a basic point about the age which we are to study. Publishers and examination boards with their fondness for labels are accustomed to call seventeenth-century Europe 'early modern'. However the more one considers France between 1610 and 1661, the more one feels that 'late medieval' would be a better description. For the realm governed by the cardinals had far more in common with France in the later middle ages than with France today. Imagine a French Rip van Winkle who fell asleep in 1350 and awoke in 1650. He would find his way around seventeenth-century France with little difficulty. But if he went to sleep again and awoke in 1950, he would be totally bewildered, for he would find modern France unrecognisable.

The reader is invited to do a Rip van Winkle in reverse and to wake up in the France of the cardinals. You have been warned that the territory to be explored will be exceedingly unfamiliar. For example, if you were to shut your eyes and awake in seventeenth-century France, the first thing that would hit you would be the stench. And it would be a different stench if you awoke in Paris or in rural Burgundy. Paris was notorious for its peculiar blend of dust, kitchen rubbish and excrement, perpetually piling up in crooked, narrow streets through which the refuse collector made occasional and ineffectual forays. In the countryside there was more space, but a similar absence of drains, latrines, and refuse collection created an appalling but different stink, especially in summer.

But the sights that would meet our eyes would be even more shocking. It would not be so much the quaint, picturesque towns still protected by their medieval walls and the ramshackle village huts of the peasants but the appearance of the people that would shake us. This would not be because of their unfamiliar clothing but because of their short stature, their faces ravaged by smallpox, teeth infections and abscesses, their limbs twisted by gout, and their whole bodies disfigured by lameness and humped backs. Poverty, malnutrition and the absence of competent medical care doomed the vast majority of French people to brief, painful and undignified lives. They would have been a sad sight by day, though not so visible by night. For another disagreeable surprise with which our eyes would have to come to terms would be the prevalence of darkness at night: no street lighting and no car headlights out of doors, and only an occasional flickering candle in the home. 'The light shining in darkness' of St.John's gospel had real meaning for our seventeenth-century ancestors.

Seventeenth-century France was an age of great intellectual darkness as well. First, it was a predominantly illiterate society. One historian has analysed 217,000 marriage contracts drawn up between 1686 and 1690 and has found that only 29 per cent of men and 14 per cent of women could sign their names. The situation earlier in the century would certainly have been worse. And the discrepancy between male and female literacy should cause us no surprise. The education of boys was bad enough. Only a minority were taught to read and write by the village priest, while an even smaller minority from the upper and middle classes received secondary education. Hardly any girls were educated beyond dressing their own hair; even aristocratic brides still played with dolls up to the time of their marriage. With this general lack of education went - inevitably - ignorance and superstition.

Perhaps the most disturbing illustration of this 'late medieval', ignorance is in the field of medicine. Louis XIII complained as he lay dying: 'I have had the unhappy lot of all prominent men - which is to be committed to the care of physicians'; and he rather unkindly remarked to his doctor, 'I would have lived longer had it not been for you'. But Louis had good reason to feel bitter. When he was two days old the membrane under his tongue had been snipped as he was apparently not sucking properly; he stammered for the rest of his life. At ten days he had a suppository rammed up his backside; he suffered both from indigestion and an anal obsession from then on. Louis' doctors and nurses inflicted further psychological damage on the little boy by perpetually dwelling on his father's sexual prowess; not surprisingly thereafter Louis was afflicted with various hang-ups, habitually exposing himself to women, experiencing strange homosexual attachments and having literally to be forced into his wife's bed. Louis XIII's poor health was a constant worry to himself and his ministers until intestinal tuberculosis completed the work which his doctors had begun. Richelieu too was a lifelong invalid and meekly allowed his doctors to torture him. On his deathbed he was finally dispatched with a prescription of white wine and horse dung. The prominent Frondeur, Cardinal de Retz, was bled remorselessly by his doctors for eight days until they killed him; he pleaded in vain for a certain English doctor who alleviated his patients' sufferings with drugs. As we turn to our own no-doubt fallible medical practitioners, who can maintain that there is no such thing as progress?

As for superstition the whole of seventeenth-century Europe experienced an Indian summer of credulity and absurdity before the scepticism and common sense of the age of reason prevailed. Perhaps the most revealing as well as the.most lurid example of such superstition was belief in the power of the black arts, which often led to the persecution of 'witches'. James I of England had an international reputation as a demonologist, while as late as 1660 the return of Stuart rule to Scotland was the signal for a backlog of witches and other deviants to be exterminated. France was not immune from this poison, especially in remote areas such as Lorraine. The particularly revealing instance of primitive, medieval superstition to which we now turn comes from Poitou, which Richelieu always felt was a little backward; even so the death of Urbain Grandier fairly exemplifies the medieval face of early modern France as a whole.

a) The Burning of Grandier - a Case Study

Canon Urbain Grandier, parish priest of Saint-Pierre, Loudon, was a fine-looking man, intelligent and charming. He was furthermore a man of courage and independence. He had led local opposition to the government's ruling that the town walls should be demolished and he had written a book questioning the rule that priests should be unmarried. Not surprisingly he was a favourite with the ladies; in fact he made a practice of cuckolding his male parishioners and fathered several bastards. Ironically it was a sexually-frustrated woman who brought about his downfall. The Mother Superior of the Ursuline Convent in Loudon was very much of a seventeenth-century type - aristocratic (her father was a friend of Richelieu's), devoid of religious vocation, sex-starved, and bored. No doubt intrigued by the vicar's reputation, she invited him to be the convent's confessor. Without giving the matter much thought, Grandier said he was too busy.

'Hell hath no fury ...'. As a result of an intrigue between the nuns and Grandier's many enemies, he was charged with sorcery. It was alleged that the nuns had become possessed by Grandier, indeed that through his satanic powers they experienced sexual intercourse with him. Grandier vehemently professed his innocence from first to last. Nevertheless he was tried, condemned, tortured and burnt alive before a vast crowd of tourists and sightseers. The nuns achieved international fame, impressing distinguished visitors from all over Europe. Wat Montagu, the Earl of Manchester's son, witnessed the Devil's final departure from the prioress' body and became a Catholic on the spot. Loudon's innkeepers and landladies made fortunes.

There are several significant aspects to this story. First is the inadequacy of the evidence by any remotely rational standards. Given that witchcraft, magic, sorcery and the like were in vogue, the charges levelled at Grandier should not surprise us. What is so striking however is that the prosecution obtained a conviction by relying on the ravings of exhibitionalist and hysterical nuns. One of the 'witnesses', Sister Claire de Razilly, drew crowds from miles around when she went into convulsions supposedly brought on by her mystical sexual relationship with Grandier; she rolled on the floor, displaying her underwear and shrieking '*Venez donc, foutez-moi*'. As for the abbess she too went into convulsions and did the splits. Subsequently when both women tried to withdraw their 'evidence', they were told that the Devil was prompting them to do this. Whereupon Sister Claire ran away while the abbess attempted suicide.

But this did not help Grandier as the trial was being managed with flagrant bias against the defendant by another typical representative of the seventeenth century, Jean-Martin de Laubardement, Cardinal Richelieu's hatchet-man. This sinister civil servant was sent to Loudon as the government's special commissioner, with instructions to 'get' Grandier. Richelieu knew that he could rely on Laubardement. The cardinal's man personally supervised the physical humiliation of the defendant - his hair, beard and moustache were shaved so that he would appear in court looking like a clown. When despite this handicap Grandier's eloquence moved the crowds of giggling women in the gallery to tears, Laubordement cleared the court. Again he personally supervised the torturing of the condemned man in a vain attempt to extract a confession of guilt. While it is true that half a century later William of Orange expressed surprise that torture was no longer used in the interrogation of suspects, it should be remembered that Grandier was tortured *after* the court had condemned him! As a French historian has pertinently commented, 'all this serves to reveal the medieval and arbitrary nature of justice in Richelieu's day'.

Why was Richelieu so anxious that Grandier should be condemned? For two 'late-medieval' reasons. First, the government had to defend its own reputation against the *dévot* party - the hard-line Catholics who were critical of Richelieu's alliances with Protestant powers (see page 48). To be seen to be 'soft' on apparent religious deviants would therefore be dangerous. A parish priest who admittedly slept around and who allegedly procured his lovers through the black arts could expect no mercy - even if he had been framed by his enemies. Secondly, Richelieu bore Canon Grandier a grudge. This again is a representative story, reminding us that to Richelieu's contemporaries status, precedence and rank meant everything. Sixteen years earlier there had been an unseemly row between Grandier and the Prior of Coussay about their respective places in a procession through the streets of Loudon. The vicar was technically right, but as events were to prove his diplomacy and common sense left much to be desired. For the Prior was also Grandier's bishop, the bishop was Richelieu and Richelieu had a long memory.

Vindictiveness, rigged trials and satanism have regularly occurred in modern times, while as recently as in the mid-nineteenth century the Lancashire and Yorkshire Railway ran excursion trains for people wishing to witness public executions. 'What this country needs is not less superstition but more superstition', argued the influential Victorian, John Henry Newman. Yet for bigoted irrationality the trial and execution of Urbain Grandier takes us back to the fifteenth-century burnings of John Hus and Joan of Arc. And Protestants tempted to indulge in self-righteousness should recall that only fifteen years before Grandier's death, Oldenbarneveldt was executed in Calvanist Holland for his belief that Christians were not necessarily predestined to hell-fire. 'Sancta simplicitas' ('holy simplemindedness') Hus exclaimed when an old peasant woman stepped forward to throw a faggot onto his fire. 'Sancta simplicitas' still prevailed as Capuchin friars sprinkled Grandier's pyre with holy water while he screamed 'God forgive my enemies'.

b) A Suffering Society

Richelieu's contemporary, the English philosopher Thomas Hobbes, described the natural life of man as 'solitary, poor, nasty, brutish and short'. This is a fair description of what life had to offer to most seventeenth-century French people. If we are shocked by 'late-medieval' superstition we should appreciate that it thrived understandably in a 'late-medieval' environment. Belief in witchcraft, sorcery and the machinations of the devil were natural responses to cataclysmic disasters against which the resources of so-called civilisation seemed to be helpless. Storms and floods can still cause havoc today. In Richelieu's France these were supplemented by plague and untimely death. We have already noted the squalor which bred disease and the medical incompetence which failed to cure it. Not only were epidemics unchecked, but countless women died in childbirth while infant mortality accounted for about half of the children who were born alive. What more natural than to resort to the prayers of priests or the spells of sorcerers in order to avert such tragedies - or to attribute them to the black magic of one's enemies? Robin Briggs has argued that witchcraft and persecution revolved round hatred and power; perhaps one should add 'suffering, ignorance and fear'.

Equally 'unmodern' was the precarious dependence of ninety per cent of the population on agriculture for survival. Despite the efforts of far-sighted ministers in charge of the French economy, such as Richelieu and Colbert, French commerce and industry languished. Indeed the truth was that there was no such thing as the French economy - simply a number of isolated local economies having minimal contact with each other. Roads were poor, communications slow, the sea infested by pirates, and internal trade stifled by countless tolls dating from the middle ages. Only a handful of places such as Paris, Lyon and Rouen would qualify as large towns by our standards. Bordeaux, La Rochelle and Marseille were prosperous ports. Otherwise so-called towns were really overgrown villages where local markets were held, and owing their importance not to trade but to the presence of a bishop or a local administrator. They were isolated islands in the vast sea of 'medieval', rural France, peopled by illiterate peasants striving to make a living out of the unsympathetic earth.

For French agriculture was desperately backward, late-medieval at best. 'Since the fourteenth century there had been no radical change in methods of farming' (G.R.R. Treasure). There was a vicious circle. Given that most stock was killed during the winter, there were too few farm animals producing too little manure, which enabled the impoverished fields to grow too few crops, which sufficed to maintain too few farm animals. Scientific stock breeding was impossible as enclosed fields were unknown. France had so few sheep that she had to import wool. Ploughs were made of wood and barely scratched the soil. Dwelling in hovels made of straw and dried mud, French peasants anxiously watched the crops ripen until the harvest was due. As a modern historian has observed, 'a wet season, a late frost, a July storm could throw an entire province into anguish and starvation'. The harvest was indeed a matter of life and death, for few peasants had any reserves on which to fall back if the harvest failed. Starvation or beggary were the only alternatives.

French peasants were further plagued by the demands of an antiquated and unjust tax system. Since the fifteenth century the king's taxes had been levied on the principle that those who could afford least contributed most. Thus the nobles were automatically exempt, the clergy contributed a pittance, the third estate - that is to say, everybody else - paid. While these unprivileged tax-payers included small landowners and townsfolk, the most numerous and the most helpless were undoubtedly the peasants. In addition, the church demanded tithe - a ten-per-cent tax which in theory supported the parish priest but which in practice usually went into the coffers of a nearby abbey. And the local landowner exacted his traditional seigniorial dues.

How grievous were these burdens? It is impossible to generalise. No doubt a bumper harvest or a mild winter made life reasonably tolerable. What can safely be said, however, is that the peasant's tax burden increased markedly under the cardinals and still further under Louis XIV due to the ruinous expense of continuous warfare. To an ever increasing extent taxes had to be collected with the assistance of soldiers - a practice which has been described as 'fiscal terrorism'. This suggests that the peasants' tax burden was indeed severe, to say nothing of their sufferings. Laubardemont (no less!) described the peasants' plight in Touraine where he was the *intendant* in a letter to Séguier the Chancellor in May 1636:

> As for the rest of my tasks, I will tell you, my lord, that the chief one is to prevent by all legitimate means the ill effects which the discontent of the populace and all the orders in general can produce, since the taxes which the necessity of the times requires are very onerous. But, my lord, the greatest evil comes from the abuses committed by those who receive the taxes and also from the troops whose violence can scarcely be described to you.

In May 1631 the king's brother, Gaston d'Orléans, gave an even more graphic description of the hardships suffered by Louis' poorer subjects:

> I have only told you what I have seen. There is scarcely a third of your peasants who eat ordinary bread; another third live on oat bread alone; the last third are not only reduced to begging but languish in such a lamentable condition that some actually die of starvation while the rest live like wild beasts surviving only on acorns, plants and such things. The least pitiful of this last group are those who eat only the husks of the grain dipped in the blood they collect from the gutters by butchers' shops. I have seen poverty such as this with my own eyes in many places since I left Paris.

Gaston went on to blame Richelieu for these appalling circumstances, and this may well have been his chief motive in writing. Nevertheless, there is corroborative evidence to suggest that he did not exaggerate.

In this medieval world of suffering, injustice and fear, what were the attitudes of the leaders of society to the disadvantaged? Basically the poor were to be knocked down or locked up. The destitute in Paris were persecuted by the 'archers of the poor' - bullies employed by the magistrates to keep potential trouble-makers off the streets. In 1661 the great Paris Hospital contained five thousand beggars, prostitutes, orphans, nursing mothers, lunatics - all lumped together for a wholesome diet of prayers, sermons, hard work and floggings. Similar institutions existed in the provinces 'to contain beggars and instruct them in piety and the Christian religion'. It should at once be admitted that such treatment of society's casualties was about par compared to the rest of contemporary 'Christian' Europe. However, a particular French characteristic was the influence of the Company of the Holy Spirit which David Parker calls 'a rather unpleasant and secretive off-shoot of the Counter-Reformation'. These *dévot* busybodies were equally concerned for the welfare of free-thinking bourgeois and suffering peasants; all were to have good done to their souls as well as their bodies. The Company's founder, the duc de Ventadour, summed up its objectives:

> Receive the unfortunate, plague stricken, convicts, peasants afflicted with gallstones or who lack seed; rescue the innocent from the provost's archers, and the debtors from the usurers' knavery; reform the dress of the Marseille women who exhibit their breasts; run freethinking bookstores into the ground; purify the St-Germain fair and gallery; attack gambling and duelling; educate teachers for elementary schools; drive out Jews and Protestants ...

d) All Doom and Gloom?

'Come on, was it that bad?' readers who have read this far may be tempted to ask. Are the horrors of life in early seventeenth century France being exaggerated in order to justify the 'late-medieval' interpretation advanced in this chapter?

Certainly there was a positive side to French civilisation and achievement in the early seventeenth century. Our Rip van Winkle friend would be surprised by many commendable developments in France between 1350 and 1650. The most striking example is the physical appearance of the country. Modern tourists are rightly impressed by beautiful buildings dating from the sixteenth century, such as the chateaux in the Loire valley. Henri IV, benefiting from this tradition, began the transformation of Paris. 'People say thet I am stingy', he remarked, 'but I do three things far removed from avarice; I make war, I make love and I make buildings'. The sixteenth century satirist Rabellais imagined his giant hero Gargantua sitting on Notre Dame Cathedral and drowning two hundred thousand Parisians by urinating on them; they could not escape through the narrow, crooked streets. Now open vistas were created, fine bridges constructed across the Seine and great palaces rose from demolished medieval slums. Provincial cities too took their cue from the capital so that the seventeenth century was to be a wonderfully productive period for French architecture. Similarly French art would flourish under the cardinals; Champaigne and Poussin would brilliantly respond to competition from foreigners such as Rubens and Van Dyke. And intellectual liveliness encouraged by Richelieu and exemplified by

Corneille and Scarron developed from the French Renaissance writers of the great sixteenth century such as the philosopher, Jean Bodin.

Nor would it be fair to belittle the achievements of the Catholic revival in France. The rejuvenated Catholicism of the seventeenth century, coherent in doctrine and flexible in its pastoral activities, proved successful in reaching widely different sectors of society. The reaction to the emergence of Protestantism was not simply to persecute. New orders were founded, attractive saints such as Vincent de Paul and Francis de Sales preached and taught, and in general the church put its own house in order. This was impressive. Perhaps such religious devotion was medieval rather than modern. However, without trespassing too far beyond the historian's province, one can at least ask whether our own secular materialism is necessarily preferable. Likewise we should note the valid argument that our modern, enlightened age which boasts Auschwitz, the gulags and the killing fields among its battle honours has nothing to learn from seventeenth century excesses. Indeed, 'medieval' is not necessarily a pejorative term.

But - to reiterate - the civilisation of seventeenth century France was so very different from that of our own day. France was a divided society to a far greater extent than we would find acceptable. While there certainly was some social mobility, the gulf between privileged and unprivileged was immense. For instance the artistic and intellectual achievements mentioned above which we rightly admire were only available to a tiny minority. With the exception of Henri IV's town planning, it was an élite culture with a vengeance. Similarly the widespread admiration for the aristocratic ideal is significant - hence the contempt for trade which so handicapped French industry and commerce to the benefit of English and Dutch rivals. Even with all his breadth of vision Cardinal Richelieu personifies this gulf between 'early modern' and truly modern. Because he regretted that aristocrats were educated only to dance, hunt and kill, he funded a college in his own town, Richelieu in Poitou, to teach the sons of noblemen the liberal arts. However, his attitude to the highly successful Jesuit schools which contained over five thousand pupils was that this was too many. Unfortunately, in his opinion, the Jesuits admitted pupils from the lower orders and gave them ideas above their station. He thought that they should concentrate instead on educating aristocrats.

In some ways it is instructive to compare Richelieu's France with England. Not that one would wish to extol or defend Stuart England as especially enlightened or progressive. It was not exactly a caring society. But in several crucial respects it really was an early-modern state where France was still essentially medieval. Thus while there was indeed a gulf between the English political nation and the rest, it was blurred and relatively easily crossed. As a perceptive observer put it, 'riches do make gentlemen in every country [county] of England'. Furthermore there was a substantial yeoman class, between the gentry and the peasants, the 'middling sort of people' who fought in Cromwell's New Model Army. There was little prejudice against gentry involvement in business and trade. Because the Anglican church never approached the Roman church's claims to a monopoly of truth, England was less regimented intellectually. Whereas in the early eighteenth century the papal bull (official pronouncement) *Unigenitus* banned the reading of the Scriptures by the laity, throughout the seventeenth century the English had free access to the Bible in the vernacular - and a highly explosive source of exciting and modern ideas it was to prove, to the discomfiture of the social and political establishment.

The contrast is most thought-provoking in the realm of politics to which we now turn. Here it might be thought my late-medieval theory will break down. Did not contemporaries regard absolute monarchy as the most enlightened, progressive and truly modern approach to government? Maybe. It is perhaps significant that Richelieu's *dévot* opponent Marillac, a real 'medievalist', condemned the cardinal's policies and argued for peace instead of war in 1629 - in order to introduce reforms in government, ease the peasants' tax burdens and, above all, persecute Protestants. Perhaps Richelieu was genuinely 'early modern'. Even so the political landscape of seventeenth-century France is indeed so strange and unfamiliar that only recently have historians begun to penetrate behind the myths of absolutist propaganda.

2 The Political Facts of Life

What were the dynamics of French government and society between 1610 and 1661? As was explained on page 2, historians used to identify the emergence of absolutism as the most important development in this period. It was argued that thanks to the political skill and determination of Richelieu and Mazarin the foundations were well and truly laid for the monarchy of Louis XIV, the Sun King. The short-sighted and selfish opposition of reactionary nobles, blinkered, bourgeois parlements and doctrinaire ecclesiastics was swept away in the cause of progress - not without some difficulty but ultimately with decisive success. The administrative infrastructure of strong royal government in the end proved too much for ineptly co-ordinated factious opposition.

However, revisionists have demonstrated that this interpretation is at best simplistic and at worst just plain wrong. France was a land of vested interests and pressure groups which were far too deeply entrenched to be defeated by a crown which lacked the coercive and administrative powers of modern dictatorships. Indeed, could there be such a thing as absolutism?

a) The Crown

In an attempt to chart a course through this controversial landscape, we can safely begin with an unquestionable and crucial landmark, the centrality of the crown. Whether royal government was absolute or not, it remained throughout a permanent and apparently indispensable feature. The French were a monarchically-minded nation. They equated the state with the crown. When Richelieu claimed that the only enemies he had were the enemies of the state, both he himself and his contemporaries would have understood 'enemies of the crown' when he spoke of 'enemies of the state'. We shall see how ministers might be detested and lampooned, tax-collectors lynched and the government's policies condemned, but no-one ever proposed that the crown should be abolished or even that the king was at fault. 'Long live the king but no gabelle (the salt-tax), let us kill the intendant and all have a piece of him!', shouted rioting peasants in Brittany.

Equally significant was the universal and heart-felt wish that the king should exert his authority. French people remembered the chaos and bloodshed of the sixteenth century religious wars, when the crown was weak. Far better that the crown should be strong. Hence the longing for a child-king to come of age - that is to say, on his thirteenth birthday. Assuming of course that the king was up to the job, public opinion was happy to see him take charge. Traditionally he commanded the armed forces, conducted relations with foreign powers both in peace and war, selected and dismissed ministers, and presided over the affairs of the French church. He was the fount of justice; while theoretically above the law, traditionally he respected it and protected his subjects' interests. Everyone felt that the realm could only be happy when the king fulfilled his responsibilities.

The French people's reverence for their king was rooted in history and myth. They were proud of the fact that rulers of France had always been French, male, legitimate and Catholic; no king of France had ever been deposed. Anointed with the oil of Clovis and descended from Saint Louis, French kings were invested with mystical powers which enabled them to heal scrofula (tuberculosis of the lymph glands) by touching the sufferer. Unlike all other laymen the king received communion in both kinds - the wine as well as the bread; this indicated his sacred, quasi-priestly status. Since the early sixteenth century the king of France had been called 'the Most Christian King' in recognition of his ancestors' services to Catholic Christianity. It was widely believed that God gave the king exceptional wisdom so that he could be a true father to his people.

Furthermore, there were thoroughly practical and prosaic reasons for the king's central role in the political life of France. If he was not the sole source of patronage, he was undoubtedly the most influential. Promotion not only at court but in the armed forces, the government and the church was in his gift. He was the fount of money and power. Rank, status, privileges were his to bestow. Even the most prestigious nobleman knew that in the last resort he was dependent on the king's favour, for the royal nod could make or break him. Needless to say these impressive powers could rebound disastrously on an unwise ruler. A weak and foolish king could be captured by faction - Louis XV's fate. An insecure, unapproachable king could alienate his nobles - Louis XIII's misfortune. But a flexible, gregarious, self-confident monarch such as Louis XIV demonstrated what a strong hand the king had if only he knew how to play it. In any case - however inept the royal wielder of patronage and power - the potential was there, and everybody knew it. When it came to promotion the king was indispensable.

b) The Nobility and Patronage

However, the absolutist myth seriously misleads with regard to the aristocracy. The argument used to be that the crown progressed from abject subordination to the nobles through conflict to ultimate triumph. It is true that the last feeble remnants of the Valois line, Charles IX (1560-1574) and Henri III (1574-1589), were undermighty kings plagued by overmighty subjects. As we shall see, Richelieu was indeed obliged to fight and win battles against France's great nobles. Louis XIV certainly dominated his blue-blooded court including such potentates as Mazarin's tormentor, Louis, prince de Condé. But recent research has shown that apparent conflict between crown and nobility ended in compromise rather than royal victory and that it was punctuated throughout with mutually profitable arrangements and alliances. For most of the time monarch and aristocracy recognised that they had far more to lose than to gain from confrontation. Certainly, in Bourbon times co-operation between the two was the norm and not the exception.

Indeed it would have been strange had it been otherwise. King and nobles shared the same cultural background, the same social privileges and prejudices, the same economic exploitation of the lower orders of society, and the same preoccupation with military affairs as the only calling fit for a gentleman. Louis XIV was an unmitigated snob, obsessed with birth, breeding and etiquette; the aristocratic life of the courtier was the only life he understood. Much the same could be said of Richelieu, the alleged hammer of the nobility. He was himself a nobleman, keen to promote the welfare of his own relations through advantageous marriages with other noble families. The last thing such men desired was the degradation of the nobility.

The fact is that seventeenth-century France was not dominated by conflict between crown and nobility but by in-fighting involving patronage and clientage. Both at the centre and in the provinces society was hierarchical, revolving round rival, aristocratically-dominated factions. Great interest groups thrived or withered depending on the manipulative skill of highly-placed patrons and the loyal support of their clients. Sharon Kettering who has analysed seventeenth-century clientage describes it as 'a blurred and boudlerised form of feudalism'. Indeed what had changed since medieval times? Only gradually was armed rebellion outlawed, while especially in remote areas barons with their armies of retainers continued to indulge in gang-warfare. In the more civilised environment of Paris and the provincial capitals great men promoted their own interests and those of their followers by more peaceful but equally ruthless means - to their mutual profit. Now there were no formal oaths of allegiance, no exchanges of feudal fiefs. Instead patrons, assisted by middlemen or brokers, established their own informal, shifting interest groups. A clever and influential patron would procure jobs in local government, plush ecclesiastical livings and prestigious marriages for his clients. On their part clients would support their patron by furthering his interests - by publicly supporting him with their physical presence, by writing, by speaking, by fighting on his behalf. It was emphatically not the era of the self-made man; it did not matter what you knew, it was who you knew that mattered.

Subordinate only to the king, the leaders of aristocratic society were the greatest patrons. Such men were provincial governors, army commanders, archbishops, royal ministers. Their time would be divided between attendance at court and involvement in local politics. A nobleman's clients would expect him to procure the king's approval for their schemes where this was necessary; so he had to know his way around court. Similarly the government would expect a nobleman to defend the king's interests in his locality; therefore he would need to keep an eye on local affairs.

An excellent example of the way patronage worked is provided by the rise of Richelieu. Due to family interest he obtained the bishopric of Luçon - 'the muddiest in France', he complained, but it was a real power-base for an ambitious ecclesiastic. Cleverly exploiting his position as a prominent member of the first estate, Richelieu became the client, or to use the contemporary word, the creature, of Concini and after his downfall, of Marie de Medici. She proved a most effective patron, procuring for her creature a place in the government and a cardinal's hat. 'This hat which I owe to your support', Richelieu assured the queen mother, 'will always remind me that I have promised to shed my blood for you'. Richelieu however now executed some nimble footwork, abandoning his former patron - to her ill-concealed rage - and becoming the king's creature in his campaign against his own mother. So much for Richelieu's promises! Shrewd, flexible exploitation of patron-client relationships was the key to the cardinal's acquisition and retention of power.

A further point however is almost as important. On his way to the top Richelieu had built up his own network of clients. In the totally carnivorous atmosphere of court politics it was essential for an ambitious politician to have supporters and assistants on whom he could confidently rely - and that they should be strategically placed. Richelieu understood this perfectly. He had his 'ears' and 'eyes' not only looking out for his interests in the king's household but also spying on his erstwhile patron, the queen mother, and indeed on the queen, Anne of Austria, who hated and feared Richelieu. 'Rotten arse' she nicknamed him, alluding to his painful ailments. The cardinal smiled grimly when such pleasantries were relayed to him. He had little cause to worry about Anne of Austria's malice, for one of his creatures was also intercepting her imprudent correspondence with her brother, the Cardinal Infante, Spanish commander-in-chief in the Netherlands. So far as real power was concerned, Richelieu had the trump cards. His team of ministers increasingly consisted of his creatures until hardly anyone was left in the government who was not dependent on the great first minister. He promoted them, they supported him.

Richelieu's exercise of patronage was not confined to politics. Like many noblemen he spotted, supported and promoted architects, artists and writers. He was a discerning patron. Le Mercier was his favourite architect; the Palais-Cardinal and the town of Richelieu illustrate his genius. Richelieu's portrait was painted several times by Champaigne (see front cover) who brilliantly conveys the pitiless determination and icy intelligence of his subject. At Richelieu's bidding Balzac wrote plays, Desmarets produced ballets, Boisrobert wrote propaganda (and stole Richelieu's books). In fact, Boisrobert is an excellent example of patronage in action. He eventually disgraced himself by hiring prostitutes to act in a play which Richelieu himself had written for performance at court. But Richelieu did not abandon his client - who as it happened was a priest. A cosy canonry was found for him in the cathedral at Rouen. Richelieu was actually a generous though perhaps to our way of thinking a somewhat quixotic patron. While Le Mercier received 3,000 livres a year as the Cardinal's architect, Richelieu paid Champaigne a mere 150 livres for the magnificent triptych portrait of the cardinal. One of Richelieu's clients commemorated the death of his great patron in the following touching words:

Ci-gît par le morbleu
Le Cardinal de Richelieu
Et ce que cause mon ennui
Ma pension avec lui.

(Here lies, dammit, Cardinal Richelieu and, what really upsets me, my pension lies here with him.)

Richelieu typified another aspect of aristocratic patronage: the domination of the provinces. The nobleman who governed a province had immense opportunities for benefiting his clients, just as he needed the support of the leaders of local society. So Richelieu obtained for himself the post of governor of Brittany - an outlying, only recently incorporated and therefore potentially troublesome part of France. But

Brittany offered great opportunities for profit and patronage to Richelieu in his capacity as Grand Master of the Marine, and he was able to promote members of his family in the Breton church and administration who in their turn would be loyal to the cardinal; for instance the deputy governor was La Meilleraye, Richelieu's cousin, who received a 'present' of 36,000 livres from the local Estates, acquired an army command and became a duke. In the same way Montmorency turned Languedoc into his personal domain, Condé dominated Burgundy and the duc de La Rochefoucauld presented 1,500 noblemen from Poitou at the siege of La Rochelle to Louis XIII: 'Sire, there is not one who is not related to me'.

To sum up, the French political scene was dominated by factions, headed by the aristocratic leaders of society, cemented by patronage. The prizes competed for included promotion in the church, the army and government. There were also fortunes to be made, for instance out of the corrupt, clumsy system of taxation and out of the various slush-funds at the disposal of ministers. Again, Richelieu illustrates this fact of life. Recent research has proved that he made vast personal profits out of the bankruptcy of the state. Truly there was much to play for in a society in which the real dynamics were ambition and greed.

c) An Ordered Society

It would be a mistake however to envisage the political society of Richelieu's France in purely vertical terms, that is to say conflict between factions embracing all the various social orders. Society was also divided horizontally, for it was a highly class-conscious, or to use the contemporary terminology, order-conscious age. There are clear examples of this order-consciousness among the many peasant revolts in the first half of the century; not only the hated tax-collectors, but parasitic bourgeois and arrogant landowners were violently attacked. Such outbursts were admittedly exceptional and sporadic, though real enough. Even more significant, however, because they were a permanent feature of French society, were the rivalries and resentments between the nobility of the sword and the nobility of the robe. Indeed it could fairly be argued that the two sections of the nobility were far more interested in fighting each other than in defying the Crown.

Members of the sword nobility prided themselves on their ancient lineage, ideally traceable back to at least the fourteenth century. They originally owed their ennoblement to military service on behalf of the crown and they continued to serve the king as soldiers - the supremely honourable profession. In recognition for their unstinting self-sacrifice on the battle-field they were exempt from taxation. By the same token they refrained from involvement in business or commerce which would distract them from their military calling and in any case was considered demeaning. The ancient nobility also traditionally served the crown in government and diplomacy, while their blue-blooded relatives monopolised the highest positions in the church. The nobleman was expected to behave like a gentleman, to live in style and to conform to the expectations of his social inferiors.

But there was another road to ennoblement. The crown could reward faithful administrators, lawyers and financiers with promotion to the ranks of the aristocracy. Such men were called the *robins* or the nobility of the robe (the judge's robe was their badge of office). As long as these lesser nobles remembered their place and did not threaten their social superiors' monopoly of power and influence, the sword nobility was reasonably content. But for a number of reasons friction occurred. First, the first three Bourbon kings increasingly employed *robins* in high office - a practice intensely resented by the sword nobility. Secondly, while inflation made a nobleman's life-style harder to maintain, recently ennobled merchants and financiers were able to afford it more comfortably than an impoverished noble of the sword. Thirdly, both the Paris and the provincial parlements gave the *robins* a forum in which to display their value to the crown and their importance in society. Although the king could legislate on his own authority by what was known as a *lit de justice,* it was recognised that both law and taxation possessed greater credibility if registered by the *parlements.* Here the robe ruled supreme.

A significant illustration of the sword nobility's values and prejudices is provided by the issue of duelling. Gentlemen settled disputes between themselves by fighting each other with sword or pistol. However, the king and his ministers were never wholly happy about duelling which could be seen as epitomising public lawlessness. Richelieu, whose elder brother had been killed in a duel, felt especially strongly that this practice should stop: 'They have constantly assumed the role of paid gladiators and have transformed the operation, the sole object of which is the destruction of human life, into a veritable art form'. But as we shall see in the next chapter, some members of the ancient nobility were even prepared to go to the scaffold in order to defend their right to duel. Why? Partly no doubt due to conservatism and arcane notions of gentlemanly behaviour. But there can be no doubt that the nobility of the sword resented Richelieu's alternative method of settling disputes, that is to say, the law. Were the ancient nobles of France to submit their disputes to the tribunals of jumped-up pen-pushers masquerading as noblemen? No way!

The ancient nobility was also threatened by a peculiarly seventeenth-century phenomenon, the sale of office. Upwardly mobile careerists or for that matter successful businessmen wanting a safe investment could purchase status and security by investing in a post in one of the many government departments, especially the law, tax-collection, and local government. Even the posts of secretaries of state - the highest in the land - had to be bought. This extraordinary system owed its origin and continued existence to the crown's ever-increasing need of money. When Richelieu came to power France contained about forty thousand office-holders all of whom had bought their positions. When death removed Mazarin from office, there were sixty thousand. Nobody pretended that these officials were actually needed. In former times that might have been the case. Now it was blatantly obvious that two men - or twelve men - did one man's job simply because they had paid the crown the going rate for appointment to the position. And the office-holders got value for money. In a status conscious society they acquired the respect accorded to government officials, irrespective of birth. They also received a regular income financed by tax-payers, and were able, in their official capacities, to help their friends. They felt that they could snap their fingers at the impoverished nobleman however ancient his lineage and however distinguished his service to the crown on the field of battle.

Historians disagree about how damaging this system was to royal government. Obviously it was inefficient and expensive. What the Crown definitely did not have at its disposal was a modern professional civil service. The office-holder was not appointed due to any qualifications or suitability, nor could he be dismissed. By the terms of the *paulette* (see page 9) he could even pass on his position to his children. However, the system worked after a fashion and it brought one unquestionable benefit to the Crown. It created a huge body of solid and respectable people whose interests coincided with the government's and who would therefore support the government. Civil disturbances, successful revolts, defiance of royal authority, foreign invasion - all such upsets could bring about a collapse of the country's political and financial establishment. If that were to happen, the office-holder could well lose his office, his income and his status. No wonder officials were almost invariably loyal to the Crown, for there was a profound community of interests between them.

Nobility of the sword, nobility of the robe, officials, the bourgeoisie of the towns, the peasants: such were the orders of a horizontally divided society. Naturally there was some movement between the orders, as families prospered, were ennobled or were disgraced, but in national terms it was insignificant. Richelieu's family was a good example of what was possible. His father was a scion of the sword, while his mother was a La Porte, a successful Parisian robe family: 'To think that I should live to see the grandson of lawyer La Porte walking into a room before the grandson of the emperor Charles V', smugly remarked Richelieu's uncle when the duke of Savoy was presented at court. Marxist historians have stressed these horizontal divisions, interpreting the rebellions of Louis XIII's reign in class terms. On the other hand, recent research has emphasised vertical groups, bound together by patronage. Popular revolts can be quoted where a nobleman led his whole province against the crown's tax-collectors; Motte de la Forêt for example in July 1636 led the bourgeoisie and the peasants of Bergerac in a well-organised rebellion.

The truth, of course, is that the vertical and horizontal interpretations of French society are not mutually exclusive. Both perceptions offer helpful insights into the politics of the time. It is certainly clear that in order to survive the Crown had to manoeuvre carefully, making the most of circumstances which reflected both horizontal and vertical divisions.

d) 'Money, Money, Money'

Nor can there be any doubt about the Crown's pressing need for cash. This was the single greatest cause of political change and administrative development under the cardinals.

There were various causes for this royal cash shortage. Partly no doubt the problem was sheer financial mismanagement; as Richard Bonney has pointed out, 'the range of talent available to fill the post of finance minister in seventeenth century France was never very great'. Then there was the highly imperfect system of tax collection. The king was lucky if he got half what he was entitled to, for tax officials were notoriously corrupt. Today we would say that the system had been privatised, in that syndicates of tax-farmers offered the crown cash for the right to extract as much as they could from the unfortunate tax-payer. The system was also illogical and unfair. Outlying provinces such as Brittany and Languedoc, known as *pays d'état,* were able to negotiate relatively light taxes, while the rest of France, the *pays d'élection,* paid through the nose. Above all the greatest cause of royal financial embarrassment was war. Rightly or wrongly the governments headed by the cardinals committed France to a long, bloody struggle against the Habsburgs which was horrendously expensive.

The precise consequences of this persistent cash shortage will emerge in the following chapters. It is sufficient here to say that in order to raise the immense sums of money which were needed, France's political leaders had to improvise and develop a complex, ever-expanding administrative machine. Modern historians describe these developments as 'the warfare state'. Although there was continuity in that this warfare state evolved from existing institutions, there was dramatic change as well. In particular, central bureaucracy became more professionalised while in the localities the government's authority was considerably strengthened by the *intendants.* Equally important was the shrewd exploitation of patronage by the Crown. As Sharon Kettering observes, 'patronage as a technique of political control and a motive for political action has been insufficiently emphasised by historians of the early modern French state'. The cardinals used these techniques in order to defeat opposition which inevitably occurred given the costs and casualties of war. Not without difficulty and not without temporary setbacks such as the Fronde, the power of royal government was markedly enhanced whether one calls it 'absolutism' or not.

Had the Crown much choice about which measures to adopt given the parameters which we have described? Possibly not. The crucial decision - and here there surely was choice - was to go to war. Given that decision and the consequent need for cash, the cardinals manoeuvred as effectively as they could. They had to take into account the socio-political dynamics which we have described. They were clever, realistic politicians. They did their best in the circumstances. Whether they fully understood the consequences of their actions, whether they took the right decisions, whether their policies benefited or harmed the French people, are questions to which the answers will emerge in the following chapters.

3 An Unhappy Couple

There is at least one unifying factor with regard to the history of France between 1610 and 1661. For better, for worse, the nation was governed in theory or in fact by one or other member of a strange marital partnership - Louis XIII and Anne of Austria. We end our account of the state of the nation with a glance at this unloving, ill-matched couple.

That dynastic marriages are seldom based on the preferences of those involved, still less on any element of love, is a statement of the obvious. An exception was Louis XIII's sister Henrietta Maria's marriage to Charles I of England; after a bumpy start this turned into a real love-match. This is ironic as there can seldom have been such a loveless marriage as that between Louis XIII and Anne of Austria. In this, as in so many other respects, the children of Henri IV had mixed fortunes.

We have already witnessed Louis XIII's sufferings at the hands of his parents and his doctors. Not surprisingly he became an unpleasant adult, mistrustful, cruel and vindictive. His hobbies were cooking - his omelettes were famous - clock-making and, above all, falconry. A particular source of pleasure for Louis was to remove pigeons' tail-feathers and hawks' talons in order to prolong the fun; in fact he used to watch such entertainment taking place in his own study. Louis was also intelligent, masterful and devoted to his task of ruling France. He was a devout Catholic who took his obligations as a king and as a Christian extremely seriously. But he was a difficult man to know and a difficult man to handle. Richelieu - who knew him better than most - used to say that he had more trouble with the six feet of the king's study than with the whole of the rest of Europe. 'I was lucky if he accepted two out of four suggestions', the cardinal used to say. Historians now believe that Louis' opinions mattered more than pro-Richelieu propaganda has suggested. Perhaps a courtier's summary got it right: 'Louis XIII wanted to be ruled, but supported being so impatiently'.

In many ways Louis XIII was precisely the monarch France needed

Anne, Queen of Louis XIII attributed to Charles Beaubrun

and deserved. He personified many of the characteristics of the society which we have analysed. He was virtuous, austere and a judgemental prude. 'Louis the Just', they called him. 'You will give me unspeakable pleasure' he wrote to Chancellor Seguier, 'by seeing to the punishment of swearing and blaspheming that are current, not just in Paris but throughout France - not to mention thefts, murders and duels'.

Anne of Austria could hardly have been less like her husband. She had had a stable, affectionate childhood and was thoroughly normal. She was not particularly intelligent, rather frivolous and totally unprepared for her role as queen when she came to France as a twelve-year-old girl. Over the years she learnt common sense and prudence. But she learnt slowly and painfully. Initially she was lonely and bewildered, longing for news of her family and contacts with her beloved Spain which she knew she would never see again. Unless, that is, she was sent home in disgrace - a fate which for much of the time she believed was by no means out of the question.

Anne and Louis did not enjoy each other's company. They went their separate ways. They seldom had sexual intercourse with each other. A rare pregnancy for Anne ended in 1622 in a manner which finally destroyed any affection or respect which Louis had for his wife. One of Anne's few sources of pleasure was the companionship of her court ladies, including the high-spirited, rather giddy duchesse de Chevreuse. This seductive trouble-maker persuaded Anne, now six weeks pregnant, to participate in a race down one of the galleries in the Louvre. Anne tripped over her dress, fell heavily - and miscarried. Louis' rage was understandable, though none the less unpleasant for his poor wife. Her *raison d'être* was to produce a son. She had let France, her husband and herself down, unforgivably. Louis banished Chevreuse from court and his wife from his heart.

Anne's trials and sufferings will appear from time to time in our story. Louis was consistently vindictive and unfair towards his wife. When he lay dying, he heard the sound of distant female laughter. 'That will be the queen', he muttered. Louis was wrong. Anne, strange to relate, was devastated by her husband's death. But it is hard to believe that it was anything but a release for both of them. Certainly for the first time in her life Anne now had the chance to be herself, to live. She also had real political power thrust upon her - as we shall see.

Because it was a monarchical age, these two strange, unhappy people were inevitably important. In other words they *mattered.* As we have seen, recent biographers have suggested that Richelieu's freedom of manoeuvre has been exaggerated, so vital were the views of his royal employer; much the same goes for Mazarin's dependence on Anne of Austria's support. It could even be argued that the title of this book gives a misleading impression. Certainly the cardinals mattered, but Louis XIII and Anne of Austria give the period much of its unity and style. Both suffered much. So did their subjects.

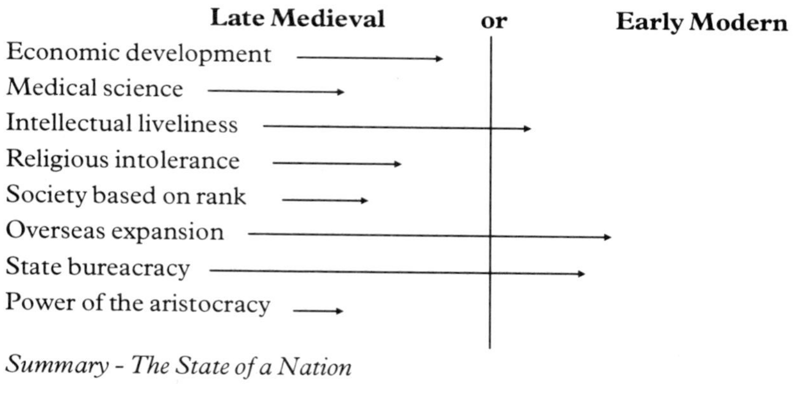

Summary - The State of a Nation

Making notes on *'The State of a Nation'*

There are various sensible approaches to making notes on a chapter like this. One is to concentrate on significant points which you feel you could well need in order to back up your arguments in essays on the policies and achievements of the two cardinals. Another good ploy is to home in on key factors such as patronage, the sale of offices or rivalry between robe and sword nobilities. If you are studying Stuart England, you could profit from a more extensive comparison than you will find here. Could the Grandier case have occurred in the England of Archbishop Laud? Was the tax system more or less efficient and just in France or England? Which monarchy had the better chance of imposing its will on the nation, the Bourbon or the Stuart? Was it preferable to be a peasant in England or France? Or you might take up my suggestion that seventeenth century France was 'late medieval' rather than 'early modern'. I may have understated the case for this suggestion! List 'medieval' and 'modern' characteristics.

Your notes on the political facts of life need to clarify the problems, opportunities and alternatives facing France's rulers. Why not try to empathise with Louis XIII, given the sort of man that he was? How would you have tackled the challenges facing the Crown? In the next chapter we shall discuss the policies adopted by Cardinal Richelieu. It will help you to arrive at a realistic assessment if you have a firm grasp of the practicalities of the exercise of power in the context in which he operated.

Answering essay questions on *'The State of a Nation'*

Again, as with chapter 1, while the material in this chapter is of value to you in answering questions on Richelieu and Mazarin, you are not likely to get many questions directly relating to the social and political scene.

> 'The reality of power belonged to the nobles rather than to the Crown in early seventeenth century France'. Do you agree with this opinion?

In your introduction show that you understand that the point of this question has to do with the controversy about absolutism. Briefly summarise the old-fashioned and the revisionist interpretations.

Your development section should marshal the arguments on the one hand in favour of aristocratic power - patronage, the prestige of the sword nobles, the increasing wealth and influence of the robe, the limitations on royal power due to distance, lack of coercive weapons and of a royal civil service. Then you should stress the potential influence of the Crown, if the hand was played skilfully.

In your conclusion come down on one side or the other. This is the kind of essay where the verdict you give will not influence the mark you get - there is after all much to be said on both sides. But you must display the necessary 'feel' for the period and you must talk sense. Above all you must give a clear answer one way or the other.

Source-based questions on *'The State of a Nation'*

How grievous were the sufferings of the French people?

Carefully read the opinions of Laubardement and Gaston (page 22) and the programme advocated by the duc de Ventadour (page 23). Answer the following questions:

a) In what ways are these descriptions of contemporary social conditions useful to historians? (7 marks)
b) How perceptive are the authors with regard to the true causes of French impoverishment? (6 marks)
c) On the evidence of these documents and of your wider reading would it be accurate to describe seventeenth century France as a caring society? (12 marks)

You could get into a dreadful mess if you failed to define 'caring society'. For the point is that in many respects France was indeed a caring society, but we might well not share the same priorities and moral values. Again this is a question where you must resist the fatal temptation to preach.

The documents do in fact indicate a certain awareness among wealthy leaders of society of the hardships of the poor. But Ventadour obviously believes that starving souls are more important than starving bodies. Do not forget to be critical of documentary sources. Laubardement no doubt aimed to impress Seguier with his conscientiousness and his compassion. Gaston was almost certainly getting at Richelieu. Nevertheless there is plenty of evidence to confirm the overall grim picture which these sources convey.

CHAPTER 3

The Ministry of Cardinal Richelieu, 1624-42

1 Introduction: the Issues at Stake

It is a tribute to Richelieu that he features far more prominently in accounts of the period 1624 to 1642 than Louis XIII, the monarch whom he served. This is no doubt partly because the king was a diffident, shy man who preferred to support his chief minister rather than take the lead himself. But it is also due to Richelieu's remarkable talents. If he was ultimately the servant and not the master of the state, he was nevertheless a very great servant who dominated not only France but Europe. Indeed one French historian claims that Richelieu 'was the greatest public servant that France ever possessed'. So part of this chapter's story is Richelieu's aims and achievements, for we must do justice to him.

However while justice undoubtedly demands a full presentation of the cardinal's creative statesmanship, blind hero-worship is no part of the historian's trade. We shall therefore note the high costs of Richelieu's policies, and we shall be concerned with his failures as well as his successes. Above all, we shall look critically at the justifications which both the great man himself and his many admirers have put forward for all the incidental suffering which he caused.

Traditionally Cardinal Richelieu has personified *raison d'état* - the idea that, whatever the consequences, every action taken to further the interests of the state can be excused. He allegedly believed in the morality of the pre-emptive strike whereby the state got its blow in first. If his policies brought torture, privation, bereavement and death to millions, Richelieu supposedly justified such mass-tragedy by pleading the interests of France. On his deathbed the great cardinal was exhorted to forgive his enemies. 'I have no enemies', he replied, 'except the enemies of the state'. Exactly! Just as he felt that he had no-one to forgive, so he believed that he had no need to be forgiven. It was all done for France.

In his book *Richelieu and Olivares* however J.H. Elliott argues that tradition oversimplifies the cardinal's priorities. Despite the fact that *raison d'état* was used by contemporaries Richelieu himself hardly ever mentioned the term. Nor would he have accepted the need for such a concept. For in his opinion there was no conflict between morality and France's interests. On the contrary it was Spain that endangered the peace of Europe, that bullied smaller states and that undermined the interests of the Catholic Church. Even France's alliances with Protestants and the grim consequences of the wars which Richelieu prolonged could be justified not only by appeals to France's interests but to the noble, Christian ideals which France defended and maintained. Clearly these assumptions would have been disputed in Madrid. But there is no reason to doubt Richelieu's sincerity or his belief in his own propaganda.

Perhaps understandably the great cardinal's admirers have preferred to quote *raison d'état* in his defence. But will even this do? Apart from the begged question as to whether Richelieu's policies did indeed benefit France, we have here the age-old conflict between morality and politics. Richelieu is not the only statesman who has caused suffering on a vast scale, supposedly in the state's interests. But as a cardinal in the Catholic church he personifies par excellence the clash between principle and expediency. Can raison d'état excuse him?

As a matter of fact, although Richelieu certainly had critics and enemies among his contemporaries, he has been generously treated by posterity. On the whole, both his alleged ability and his loyalty to French interests have been accepted with very few reservations. This is partly because Richelieu was an effective self-publicist. As we shall see, his attitude to public opinion was sophisticated, for he was one of the first of the modern media manipulators. The cardinal's *Mémoires* and his *Testament Politique,* both of which he almost certainly did not write but which he probably inspired, convey his side of the argument. Historians have accepted Richelieu as a ruthless authoritarian who nevertheless subordinated everything to France's true interests. To his own countrymen he is *the* patriotic hero. With less excuse Anglo-Saxons have been equally uncritical, welcoming Richelieu to the anti-Spanish club alongside such Protestant heroes as Elizabeth I and Cromwell. After all, did not Richelieu tolerate Huguenots? Compared to his English contemporaries, the feeble Stuart kings and their bumbling ministers, Richelieu impresses by his apparent efficiency and devotion to the public weal.

In this chapter Richelieu's policies and achievements will be critically scrutinised. Maybe he was as high-principled as he claimed and as statesmanlike, successful and disinterested as his admirers allege. But there is no harm in a little judicious scepticism. Certainly we must first establish Richelieu's objectives with their implications for France and Europe, and recognise his considerable achievements. But we must also question whether his policies really were in France's interests and whether the human and material costs really had to be so high. Similarly, though the historian must not play God, we cannot totally exclude moral issues when we assess Richelieu's record. Readers will be presented with the evidence and will be invited to decide whether Richelieu deserves the adulation and respect which he has received.

2 The Essential Richelieu

First, what made Richelieu tick? In order to arrive at a balanced judgement, we must understand this proud, withdrawn ecclesiastic whose pain-wracked eyes stare at us from Champaigne's regal portrait (see front cover). What was his background? What were his priorities and ideals? Did he have weaknesses as well as strengths? How did he come to power? What was the programme which he proposed to implement when he became chief minister? We must get the essential Richelieu right.

While it used to be thought that Richelieu's rise to high office was inevitable due to his indisputable and therefore unstoppable ability, historians now question whether the outcome was quite so pre-ordained. Armand du Plessis de Richelieu was born in Paris on 9 September 1585, the third son of François du Plessis de Richelieu of the sword nobility and Suzanne de la Porte, daughter of a prosperous Parisian lawyer. At his christening his cot carried the motto, 'Armand for the king' - prophetic words. The boy was fortunate in his father's successful track-record as marshal of Henry III's court - a post which involved him in the king's legal disputes, the organisation of provisions, and supervision of the 'daughters of joy', the prostitutes who met the courtiers' needs. Richelieu's brother was a respected soldier who perished at a duellist's hand in 1619. Until then Armand was known as 'Henri de Richelieu's brother'. We have seen (page 28) how necessary to Richelieu was first Concini's and then the queen mother's support - and how nimbly he deserted his patrons when they could no longer help him. In addition, historians have now established how useful his career in the church was to Richelieu. The bishopric of Luçon was his first power-base and he exploited his rank as a cardinal to claim precedence over his fellow ministers and to be addressed as 'my cousin' by the king. Richelieu experienced mixed fortunes on his way to the top. He learnt the value of caution and dissimulation. He got there in the end through the usual mixture of ability and luck.

Nature dealt Richelieu a mixed hand. No-one questions his powerful intellect. Although like the rest of us he made mistakes, he certainly deserves his reputation for political shrewdness. Furthermore his imagination ranged widely. He grasped the importance of colonies in the New World and he is rightly credited with the foundation of France's navy. He was a keen patron of the arts, writing and producing his own plays. He took a discerning interest in gardens, and not only supervised the construction of palaces and castles but also planned the lay-out of Richelieu, his home town in Poitou. On the other hand, he achieved all that he did despite wretched ill-health. He suffered from migraines which prostrated him for days, he was a martyr to haemorrhoids for which he once procured the relics of a saint, while bad circulation inflicted chilblains, boils and suppurating sores. Chronic indigestion and persistent insomnia were compounded by Richelieu's doctors who remorselessly bled and purged him; 'my physicians tell me that I am getting better', he wrote, 'but I cannot say that I have noticed'.

Furthermore he was emotionally and psychologically vulnerable. There was madness in the family. Richelieu's brother Alphonse, a Carthusian monk, announced that he was Christ, while his sister would never sit down because she was convinced that her buttocks were made of glass. While Richelieu was sane enough, he lived on his nerves, wept easily ('whenever he wants', sneered the queen-mother) and was often close to panic, desperately needing the support of his friends.

Not that the cardinal had many friends. He loved his niece and he was close to his unofficial foreign affairs expert, the Capuchin Father Joseph. The members of his ministerial team trusted and respected him, while Louis XIII certainly appreciated his loyalty and ability. Just occasionally the mask of icy, calculated superiority slipped, revealing a gift for friendship and a sense of humour. He bestowed affectionate nick-names on Father Joseph ('Tenebroso-Cavernoso', meaning 'darkly-inscrutable) and on Mazarin ('Nunzinicardo', meaning 'dear little nunzio') who was able to make him laugh. Richelieu got on well with cats. Otherwise he was loathed and feared. Unnatural powers were attributed to him. He was supposed to have hypnotic eyes and to be gifted with second sight. Anne of Austria was not the only person to be terrified of him.

What are we to make of Richelieu's ideals? How genuine was his devotion to France? How deep was his religious commitment? However ruthless and unlovable, was he a man of genuine principle? Richelieu is a difficult man to get to know. We shall learn what we can from his career in the king's service, evaluating his devotion to France as the story unfolds. As for his commitment to religion, we may or may not be shocked by a British historian's discovery that 'Monsieur de Luçon' was treated for 'gonnorhoea inveterata' before leaving Paris for his diocese, where as a matter of fact he proved to be a model, reforming bishop. Certainly great moral issues are raised by Richelieu's responsibility for war. How could he reconcile his belligerency with his role as a Christian priest? Another area of criticism is his pursuit of wealth. It appears that while he presided over the bankruptcy of France, he himself amassed a personal fortune of 22 million livres. In his speech to the Estates General in 1614 he recommended priests for the major offices of state because without wives and children to maintain they were uninterested in money; yet his own behaviour hardly supported this argument. Perhaps at this stage we should simply note the questions which arise concerning the cardinal's ideals and suspend judgement until the end of the story.

One quality at least neither contemporaries nor posterity have begrudged Richelieu. It is agreed that more than most politicians he pursued clearly defined goals. While he could not predict the future in detail and was more of an opportunist than he admitted, he had a definite programme based on a rational perception of France's needs. As soon as he became chief minister he recommended to his royal master the implementation of this programme. His overriding priority was the preservation of French security which he believed to be menaced by Habsburg imperialism. He was convinced that this threat could only be scotched by expensive diplomacy and ultimately by a major European war. He knew that the cost to France was bound to be high, both in terms of men and money. Suffering and deprivation - or blood, sweat and tears - would be Richelieu's gift to the French people. These only too predictable consequences would have profound implications for the political and adminstrative development of France.

Given the primacy of foreign policy in Richelieu's mind - or, expressed differently, given that his domestic policy was foreign policy-led - we shall deal first with his approach to international relations. Then we shall explore the impact of his foreign policy on French politics and society. It is a complex story, one development leading inexorably to another. Thus our first concern after exploring the cardinal's foreign policy will be his conflict with organised opposition at home, often prompted by news from abroad. The measures by which Richelieu defeated challenges to his master's and his own authority must be identified. Next we shall examine the economy which supported the ever-soaring expenses of Richelieu's wars. How were taxes raised and what if taxation failed to provide enough? How was cash extracted from an impoverished and discontented people and how were desperate and spontaneous obstruction and defiance overcome? How did royal government accomplish this goal? Having answered these questions we can proceed to an assessment of the great man's record.

3 Richelieu's Foreign Policy

As we have seen, France's foreign policy during Richelieu's tenure of power had one over-riding aim: to cut the Habsburgs down to size. This was perceived as an absolute necessity for the sake of French safety. The argument was that France was 'encircled' by Habsburg Spain and Italy to the south and south-east, the Spanish Netherlands to the north-west, and the territory of the Austrian Habsburgs and of the Holy Roman Empire, which they dominated, to the east and north-east. (See map on page 123).

The recent history of France demonstrated how serious this threat could be. In the first half of the sixteenth century the Emperor Charles V had controlled all the Habsburg lands including Spain. The power which he exercised represented a nightmare for France's rulers, Francis I (1515-47) and Henry II (1547-59), who fought a succession of wars in a vain attempt to redress the European balance of power in France's favour. In the end it was Charles himself who divided his lands between his son and his brother, one becoming King of Spain, the other Holy Roman Emperor. However, this division by no means ended the Habsburg threat. Spanish troops were concentrated in the Netherlands during the reign of Philip II (1555-98) to repress the revolt of the northern provinces. They failed to do this, but intervened against the French crown from time to time during the wars of religion (1559-98). A twelve year truce between Spain and the United Provinces (the Dutch rebel states) ended in 1621. In 1625 Spanish troops under their able general Spinola captured the key fortress of Breda. An unstable situation here was mirrored by a volatile state of affairs in Germany where the Habsburg emperor Ferdinand II had won impressive victories against the German Protestant princes - with Spanish assistance. These events spelt trouble for France.

Richelieu's so-called foreign policy therefore was in practice a war policy. Everything hinged on the outcome of the Thirty Years War raging in Europe (see page 12). By diplomacy, indirect intervention (in other words by paying others to fight on France's behalf), and finally by direct intervention Richelieu prolonged the war in an effort to prevent an extension of Habsburg power. It is impossible to understand France's achievements when she finally emerged from the shadows unless the earlier stages of the war are clearly understood, though superficially this story may not seem to have much to do with Richelieu. But in fact appearances are deceptive, for under his leadership France played a crucial role throughout.

a) First Moves

It will be recalled that Richelieu's predecessors had made ineffectual attempts to check the alarming growth of Habsburg power and influence. For instance a marriage alliance had been negotiated between Louis XIII's sister Henrietta Maria and Charles, Prince of Wales. The idea was to extract improved conditions for English Catholics and at the same time prevent England becoming a Spanish satellite. This was by no means an impossibility as James I was keen on a Spanish marriage for 'Baby Charles' despite the outraged reactions of his Protestant subjects. Meanwhile, La Vieuville (see page 12) negotiated an offensive and defensive alliance with the Dutch and tried to checkmate Spanish attempts to dominate the strategically vital areas of northern Italy.

It fell to Richelieu to finalise arrangements for the English marriage. Through no fault of his own things did not go very well. La Vieuville had failed to extract precise terms on behalf of English Catholics so that in the event nothing could be done for them. As for the recruitment of England into the anti-Spanish camp, Charles I who had just succeeded his father seemed enthusiastic. In May 1625 he sent his favourite the Duke of Buckingham to bring the bride home and sign an Anglo-French alliance against Spain. This was going too fast for Richelieu who counselled Louis XIII to reject the duke's proposal as premature. France was not ready for war.

However, Richelieu could not be blamed for the rather unconventional English reaction. Buckingham responded to France's negative attitude by making a pass at the queen. Did Anne encourage him? Neglected by her frigid and unloving husband, she may well have succumbed to Buckingham's flashy charms. What exactly happened? Not much, in all probability. Buckingham may have put his arm round her and kissed her. Louis was understandably furious, Anne was terrified of her husband's reaction, and Buckingham was indignant when he was asked to leave forthwith. And Richelieu? Years later he introduced Mazarin to Anne with the words, 'You will like him, he looks like Buckingham'. The cardinal may well have derived malicious amusement from this embarrassing affair - but it fell to him to pick up the pieces.

For there was nothing funny about the worsening relations which now developed between England and France. The fault was mainly England's. Buckingham was keen to gain revenge for the 'outrageous' way in which he had been treated, while Charles, as yet on bad terms with his young French wife, made no attempt to restrain his favourite. So Buckingham led an expedition to help the Huguenots of La Rochelle. In the next section we shall see how seriously Richelieu took this challenge to his master's authority. He made the expulsion of the English and the total defeat of the Huguenots an absolute priority, personally supervising the campaign. An ambitious anti-Habsburg foreign policy was out of the question for Richelieu as long as the Huguenots retained their capacity to make trouble at home. And there was also an alarming shortage of the cash needed to fund a major campaign.

So Richelieu's initial measures which he directed against Spain were cautious, involving relatively small-scale military initiatives in northern Italy. The rationale behind this policy was to cut the roads between Spanish Milan, a productive recruiting area, and northern Europe. In particular Richelieu tried to ensure that the Valtelline Pass was in reliable hands. A glance at the map on page 123 will reveal how crucial the Valtelline was to both French and Spanish ambitions. Spanish reinforcements for the emperor travelled that way, and so did French assistance for their ally Venice. If the 'Spanish road' from Italy to the Netherlands and Germany could be dominated by France and her allies, the threat of Habsburg encirclement would diminish. In carefully planned exercises of limited commitment French and Swiss troops expelled pro-Spanish papal troops from the pass in November 1624, and in March 1625 France and Savoy attacked Spain's ally Genoa in order to stop Spanish troop movements through the Valtelline. But that was as far as Richelieu wished to go. In the following year a compromise was reached over the Valtelline by the Treaty of Monzón; the Spanish accepted the sovereignty of the Protestant Grisson cantons over the Valtelline, while France withdrew her troops. This led to a Franco-Spanish alliance against England (20 March 1627) as a result of which Spain sent ships to help the French navy defeat Buckingham's ill-fated expedition to La Rochelle.

However, friendship between France and Spain was disrupted by the death of the Duke of Mantua in December 1627. His lands, which included the key fortress of Casale dominating the Po valley (see the map on page 123), were claimed by the Duke of Nevers, a French stooge. Strictly speaking Nevers should have consulted the emperor as Mantua was an imperial fief (part of the Holy Roman Empire). In the event he acted first by occupying Mantua and then pleaded his case with Ferdinand II. The Spaniards now intervened in this strategically sensitive area by besieging Casale. In spring 1629 French troops led by Louis XIII and Richelieu ravaged Savoy, Spain's ally, and raised the siege of Casale.

Richelieu capitalised on this success. He supervised the capture of the strategically important fortress of Pinerolo in March 1630. This prompted the threat of a major imperial and Spanish reaction; Spinola was soon besieging Casale, and Mantua fell to the imperialists. French troops rushed to the relief of Casale. However, the impending battle was prevented by an intrepid horseman who galloped between the lines shouting 'Stop! Stop! Peace! Peace!'. His name was Jules Mazarin, he was a diplomat in the Papal service and he had negotiated terms. By the Treaty of Cherasco (July 1630) Nevers kept Mantua and Montferrat while the French evacuated Casale and returned Pinerolo to Savoy. However, this last concession was only temporary as the Duke of Savoy had secretly agreed to sell Pinerolo back to France.

The capture of Pinerolo brought home to Richelieu the implications of taking on the Spaniards and the imperialists. In a cogent memorandum he put the stark alternatives before Louis XIII - surrender Pinerolo for the sake of peace, or hold on to it and accept the consequences:

> Pinerolo is taken. It is impossible fully to describe the importance of this conquest. The question consists in examining whether it is better to buy a peace by giving up Pinerolo or to conserve it in a long war ... As to whether or not money is sufficient, that depends on Monsieur the finance minister, who must reckon for this army's subsistence that we must have every three months 1.8 million livres. If my opinion is asked for, the place where I am now (Pinerolo) prevents me from giving it. All I can say is that if it is kept and refurbished, the king will be arbiter and master of Italy. If on the other hand it is returned, he must forget about Italy for ever. If the king decides on war, it will be necessary to give up all thought of tranquility, retrenchment and of reform inside the kingdom.

For all Richelieu's protestations of unbiased detachment, his preferences were clear enough. In the event Louis followed the cardinal's lead and chose war. This was a very significant decision because recent developments further north clearly indicated how high the cost of confrontation with the Habsburgs would certainly be. In 1630 the king of Spain and the Emperor were on the crest of a truly impressive wave.

Everything had gone well for the Habsburgs. Not only had the Spaniards conquered the Palatinate, dangerously close to France's eastern frontier, but in addition the imperialists had carried all before them. Desperately worried about their security, the Dutch had allied with Christian IV of Denmark. A soldier of fortune, Count Mansfeld, who had a huge private army at his back, had been hired by the Dutch. 'God help those where Mansfeld comes', was the contemporary saying. In truth Mansfeld created greater problems for his friends than for his enemies. At Lutter in 1626 the combined Danish and mercenary armies were defeated by the imperialist general Tilly and in the following year chased out of Germany. Another of Ferdinand's generals, the dangerously ambitious Albrecht von Wallenstein, had completed the conquest of Bohemia and now added Mecklenberg to the emperor's dominions. Ferdinand was master of central Europe, from Prague to the Baltic. In the summer of 1630 he confidently summoned the Electors (the German princes who had the right to choose the emperor when there was a vacancy) to an imperial diet (meeting) at Regensburg. His particular purpose was to get his son elected King of the Romans - the courtesy title which belonged to the unquestioned heir to the empire. Such a triumph would set the seal on a decade of Habsburg successes.

Among the representatives of foreign powers at Regensburg were two Frenchmen: Brûlart de Léon, the official leader of the delegation, and his 'theological adviser', the Capuchin friar Joseph du Tremblay. Better known as Father Joseph this ascetic aristocrat was Richelieu's close friend. He was as fanatical an opponent of Habsburg hegemony as Richelieu, though for characteristically bizarre reasons. Father Joseph dreamt of a crusade to liberate the Holy Land from the Turkish infidels. Since his attempts to preach his crusade at Madrid had fallen on deaf ears, the King of France would have to lead it. For the crusade to succeed, a united Christendom was essential, including a conquered and chastened Spain acknowledging the leadership of Father Joseph's master, 'the Most Christian King'. Thus did the Capuchin justify France's defiance of Catholic Spain.

Father Joseph was completely in Richelieu's confidence. He had secret instructions to prevent the election of the emperor's son as King of the Romans and to recruit as France's allies the Electoral Princes, especially the Elector of Bavaria. As it happened, Father Joseph's job had been made easier by the emperor's successes which thoroughly alarmed all the German princes. The Protestants were appalled by the Edict of Restitution which Ferdinand had just issued, ordering the return to the Catholic church of all land taken from it since 1552. So the Electors were easily persuaded to vote against Ferdinand's son. They also delighted Father Joseph and Richelieu by persuading the emperor to dismiss Wallenstein and to accept the settlement of Italian affairs embodied in the Treaty of Cherasco. In addition a Franco-Bavarian alliance was signed in May 1631, as a result of Father Joseph's diplomacy. Well might the emperor remark: 'a poor Capuchin has disarmed me with his rosary and has managed, despite the narrowness of his cowl, to stuff six electoral bonnets into it'.

Although Richelieu churlishly maintained that a better settlement of Italian affairs could have been achieved, Father Joseph returned from Regensburg in triumph. France had established herself as the protector of the German princes and their precious 'liberty' (privileges) against Habsburg imperialism. But Richelieu knew that there was a limit to what diplomacy could accomplish. Ultimately France could only be saved from Habsburg encirclement by military means. The French army was not yet ready for a major European war. Salvation would have to come from the north where a deliverer was poised ready to intervene.

b) The Swedish Intervention

The great captains of the Thirty Years War numbered several eccentrics. These included Wallenstein the slave to astrology, perpetually consulting his horoscope, and Mansfeld who in his mortal illness got out of bed and met death standing up, in full armour. But none was stranger than King Gustavus Adolphus of Sweden. This flaxen-haired, myopic commander of men who invented the modern cavalry charge was a military genius. His physical courage was legendary. Oblivious to danger he led from the front. 'What is the use of a king in a box?' he asked when his advisers remonstrated with him over his disregard for his own safety. 'He thinks the ship cannot sink that carries him', one contemporary observed, referring to 'Evangelical Joshua's (one of Gustavus Adolphus's nicknames) belief in God's protection. His men worshipped him and would follow him anywhere.

This Protestant warlord was the unlikely ally whom Richelieu recruited for his anti-Habsburg crusade. By the Treaty of Bärwalde (January 1631) negotiated on France's behalf by the baron de Charnacé, Gustavus agreed to invade Germany with 30.000 infantry and 6,000 cavalry in return for a million livres a year for five years. He also promised to respect Catholic worship and not to attack Bavaria if she remained neutral. Thus did Richelieu attempt to reconcile his agreements with his Catholic friends in Germany and his Protestant champion from Sweden. Actually Richelieu seriously misread Gustavus if he thought that his new ally would meekly obey the King of France and his cardinal; events were to prove that he who paid this particular piper did not call the tune. Gustavus gladly accepted French money which tided him over temporary financial difficulties. But he had his own reasons for intervening in Germany. He personified Swedish imperialism in his anxiety to dominate the southern shore of the Baltic. And he saw himself as the God-appointed saviour of German Protestantism.

Whether the German Protestants wanted to be saved by Gustavus Adolphus was another matter. However, the imperialists played into his hands. First, the leading Protestant Electors John George of Saxony and George William of Brandenburg failed to persuade the emperor to withdraw the Edict of Restitution; if he had done so, they would have helped him resist the Swedes. Secondly, the imperialist army led by Tilly perpetrated the worst atrocity of an atrocious war, the sack of Magdeburg. The German Protestants rallied to Gustavus Adolphus. Fired with indignation he swept through northern Germany like an avenging angel. On 17 September 1631 one of the decisive battles of the century, the battle of Breitenfeld, took place. Gustavus, the 'Lion of the North', annihilated the imperialists. Germany lay at his feet.

And Gustavus had every intention of making the most of his victory. The Saxons were dispatched to restore Protestantism in Bohemia, while 'Evangelical Joshua' led the Swedes through Franconia and Thuringia into the Rhineland, helping himself to the possessions of Richelieu's Catholic allies. 'Control your bloodhound!' they shrieked. But Richelieu now discovered that he could not do this, for Gustavus humiliated a French delegation led by Richelieu's nephew de Brézé requesting him to evacuate the Rhineland. All the French could do was to invade Lorraine to protect their own eastern frontier from their Swedish ally. In spring 1632 after Maximilian provoked Gustavus by recapturing Bamberg, the Swedes invaded Bavaria. When Gustavus swept into Munich like Christ purging the temple, Richelieu was in despair.

But not for the first or the last time luck came to the cardinal's rescue. Since the Emperor Ferdinand had now recalled Wallenstein, the imperialists could again field a sizeable army. A titanic battle took place at Lutzen on November 16 1632. Once again the imperialists were thrashed. But the 'Lion of the North' was slain, typically leading his cavalry into the thick of the action. Thus was Richelieu relieved of his insubordinate mercenary. Indeed the fact that Gustavus was shot in the back gave rise to rumours that the resourceful cardinal had had the Swedish king assassinated. This has never been proved, but the king's death was certainly convenient and the rumour was a tribute to Richelieu's international reputation for skulduggery.

Actually Richelieu was hard to satisfy. He heartlessly wrote to Louis XIII: 'If the King of Sweden had postponed his death by six months, it seems likely that Your Majesty's affairs would have been more secure'. Certainly France's problems were by no means over. Richelieu's attempt to champion German liberties had looked increasingly threadbare while Gustavus rampaged unchecked. Now that he was dead the Catholic princes threw in their lot with the emperor. So it was only the Protestants whom Richelieu was able to keep in line. At Heilbronn they agreed to continue the war in alliance with the Swedes now led by the regent Axel Oxenstierna.

Richelieu played his cards cautiously as the imperialists and the Spanish prepared for a final showdown. He completed the occupation of Lorraine, and tussled with the Swedes in seizing key towns in Alsace such as Philippsburg. In addition, in early 1634 he advised Louis XIII to reject approaches first from the Dutch and then from the Swedes for overt military alliances. Maybe his caution was justified. But possibly a bolder policy might have averted the disaster which now ensued. Anne of Austria's brother the Cardinal Infante assembled a formidable army in Milan with which he proposed to intervene in the Netherlands. Because the route through Alsace and Lorraine was now in French hands, he moved through the Valtelline into Germany. At Nördlingen on 6 September 1634 the Spanish army utterly defeated the Protestant army of the League of Heilbronn. Once again the Habsburgs were triumphant.

Robin Briggs has argued that the Spanish would have benefited in the long term from losing the battle of Nördlingen. If they had been defeated they would almost certainly have had to withdraw from the conflict in northern Europe. Then they could have consolidated their hold on their empire and saved themselves from another quarter century of debilitating warfare. It is a plausible argument. What cannot be doubted is that Nördlingen was a major catastrophe for Richelieu. All his plans now lay in ruins. His attempts to defeat the Habsburgs by proxy without actually involving France had led to the domination of Europe by the Spanish. Now only direct intervention by France could turn the tables. Contrary to the myth that Richelieu with brilliant intelligence fought the war with German and Swedish blood until France was ready to fight, France was certainly not ready - as the next few months' campaigning would prove. Furthermore Richelieu was now starkly and uncomfortably displayed as the saviour of European Protestantism - a peculiar situation for the cardinal chief minister of Catholic France. As William of Hesse Kassel remarked, 'The House of Austria wishes to subjugate all Germany extirpating liberty and the Reformed religion. So in this extremity we must look to France'.

c) France at War, 1635-42

During the last seven years of his ministry Richelieu was the most hated man in France. Even the king's support could not be assumed, for given that Louis XIII expected results, a series of defeats would inevitably put his chief minister's job at risk. As we shall see in the next section, Richelieu's war caused France acute suffering at home. Direct involvement in the fighting was inevitably unpopular, as was the cardinal's co-operation with Protestants. For France was now allied with the Dutch and the Swedes, while Richelieu recruited thousands of Protestant Germans into the French army: 'To levy so many Huguenots

[Richelieu's word] is vexatious, but few good men are to be found'. The *dévots* never forgave him. And to make matters worse, he did not achieve the victory which would have justified him.

Richelieu insisted that France should declare war on Spain and not on the emperor, and that the official notification should be delivered by a herald to the Cardinal Infante in Brussels (May 1635). However, the Spaniards and the imperialists co-operated closely. Before long the Protestant Electors sued for terms. The Swedes had no wish to fight the Spaniards and refused to co-operate with France. Soon France was isolated. The very situation which Richelieu had dreaded had come to pass. France lay at the mercy of the encircling Habsburg powers.

The French army was in no condition to meet this challenge. It was badly led, uncoordinated and ill-disciplined. There was never enough money to supply or to pay the troops. So they had to live off the land by extortion and looting, and in the early stages of the war 'the land' meant France. Richelieu was open-eyed about the quality to be expected of France's inexperienced armies compared to the battle-hardened Spaniards and imperialists. His assessment proved only too accurate as the English mercenary Sydnam Poyntz reported:

> The French army was the goodliest sight that ever I beheld, a world of brave horse and men coming up a hill in such order: and the first day they were clad all in horsemen's coats of scarlet colour and silver lace; the next day having laid by their coats they were all in bright armour and great feathers wonderful beautiful to behold. The winter coming on, either side retreated, but the French rose first, by reason the French could not endure such hardness as the Germans: but all their bravery which they showed at their coming was gone, we could see at their parting neither scarlet coats nor feathers, but sneaked and stole away by little and little from their camp. And it seems most of their brave horses were eaten or dead for few we could see at their departure nor hear so much neighing of horses as when they came.

In 1636 France reached her nadir. It was known as 'the year of Corbie'. The imperialists invaded Burgundy, the Spaniards Picardy. There was little resistance. The Cardinal-Infante captured Corbie, only eighty miles from Paris, and his cavalry reached Compiègne. There was panic in Paris. Thousands of Parisians fled to the south, just as their descendants were to do in June 1940 when Hitler's panzers swept across northern France. At a council meeting Richelieu recommended that the government should retreat to the Loire. But this was Louis XIII's finest hour. He rejected his chief minister's advice and left for the front. Under his command the French army recaptured Corbie, and the crisis passed. But it was all too much for Richelieu. He panicked, wept, and collapsed. 'Stop running about like a wet hen!' remonstrated Father Joseph.

Richelieu pulled himself together and braved the streets of Paris, reassuring the citizens that all was well, even if in his heart he did not believe it.

However, very slowly the tide began to turn. Several factors worked in France's favour. The navy won crucial victories led by Sourdis, Archbishop of Bordeaux. In 1639 the Dutch under Tromp destroyed a huge Spanish fleet sheltering off the Sussex coast. Richelieu's latest mercenary, Bernard of Saxe-Weimar, besieged the key fortress of Breisach in December 1638 as Father Joseph lay dying. 'Breisach est à nous!' lied Richelieu to comfort his friend's last hours - but it fell a few days later. When Bernard tactlessly showed signs of retaining his conquest, death providentially removed him. In September 1640 d'Harcourt redressed the balance of power in Italy in France's favour by restoring Louis XIII's promiscuous sister Christina to the throne of Savoy. While France was seething with discontent and plots germinated against Richelieu, Spain was in a worse state. In 1640 Catalonia and Portugal revolted. Olivares put out peace feelers which Richelieu, confident that his enemies were on the run, rejected. In 1641 the Emperor Ferdinand III who had succeeded his father in 1637 also indicated his willingness to discuss terms. With hindsight we can appreciate that the Habsburgs had over-reached themselves and that their ambitions had been checked. Contemporaries dared to hope that peace would some day be achieved.

But it would be wrong to exaggerate the contribution of France's armies to this upturn in her fortunes. Historians used to stress the importance of the reorganisation of military administration by Richelieu's secretary of state for war, Sublet de Noyers. Similarly it used to be argued that the slow but sure domination of aristocratic commanders by royal *intendants* made possible centralised direction of the war by the government. These reforms are supposed to have brought about French victories. However, recent scholarship has emphasised the continuing shambolic state of the French armies. To compete with the Spanish army of around 80,000 men, France's 20,000 in 1635 was clearly inadequate. Richelieu could only bridge the gap by commissioning more and more aristocratic officers who were empowered to raise their own detachments at the government's expense. This was a futile attempt to retain some control over the supposedly royal army. It would have been better had Richelieu displayed the realism of other contemporary rulers and employed military entrepreneurs with *carte blanche* to run their armies at a profit in any way they pleased. But as it was he fell between two stools. He neither had a properly controlled royal army, nor could he rely on his commanders to be self-financing.

The result was an expensive, corrupt shambles. Significantly there was always an overabundance of candidates for commissions. This was not simply because soldiering was the only honourable profession; it was also because it was profitable. The favourite ploy of the royal commanders was to cheat the king by 'borrowing' troops from other regiments or by temporarily recruiting local peasants to swell their numbers when a royal commisssioner inspected the muster rolls. *Intendants* complained that commanders openly boasted of their success in cheating the government. Far from dominating the generals the *intendants* could only exercise control through conniving at abuses. Nor could they force officers to accept military discipline and obey orders any more than they could prevent them abandoning their troops and sloping off to Paris whenever campaigning got tough.

How did such an army achieve any success at all? What about Condé's celebrated victory at Rocroi in 1643 (see page 89) which Richelieu did not live to see but which apparently vindicated his methods? Historians now regard Rocroi as sudden and unexpected - in fact a total fluke. They point out that apart from Rocroi the French army achieved no decisive victories until Cromwell's redcoats helped them win the battle of the Dunes in 1658. All that can be claimed for Richelieu's armies is that the Spanish failed to knock them out. It was really a conflict between two exhausted giants, of whom France was able to remain upright longer. As it was, the peace which Richelieu professed to desire seemed to recede ever further into the distance. While he grappled with intrigue at home and suffered the tortures of ill-health, his last days cannot have been happy.

Nevertheless in a sense the cardinal had achieved his aims. The Habsburgs were checked, even if they were not finally defeated. The necessary spade-work had been accomplished for ultimate victory. France was now established as the protector of the German princes with her bridgeheads on the Rhine. To the south Rousillon had been annexed, and on the vulnerable eastern frontier Lorraine had been occupied. A power vacuum was developing in Europe which France could eventually exploit. For Sweden's bid for European hegemony had failed and Germany was devastated. As for England, Richelieu shrewdly advised Louis XIII not to assist his brother-in-law Charles I against parliament, for the cardinal knew a loser when he saw one. In any case, the distraction of civil war would remove another possible rival to French domination of Europe. *La grande siècle* beckoned. But at what cost?

4 The War against the Enemy Within France

We have now established that the foreign policy adopted by Louis XIII and his cardinal involved France in war - first indirectly on a limited scale and then from 1635 onwards in direct and bloody confrontation with the Habsburg powers. The cost to France was immense: for thousands death, for tens of thousands suffering from wounds and bereavement, for whole provinces invasion by the enemy or, what was often worse, occupation by the French army, and for everyone the burdens of high taxes. Inevitably the government became intensely unpopular, its authority was challenged, its priorities were questioned. As we have seen Richelieu responded to this defiance by creating the 'warfare state'. He met criticism and opposition head on, vastly increasing the coercive authority of the crown, creating the necessary political and administrative machinery to extract taxation and beat down opposition, and assailing his critics with tendentious propaganda. In the words of a contemporary, 'Richelieu blasted rather than governed the king's subjects'.

Historians used to argue that Richelieu implemented a carefully planned programme in his campaign to strengthen royal authority. This programme allegedly demanded first of all the defeat of three potential sources of domestic defiance - the Huguenots, the nobility and the *parlements.* Certainly Richelieu himself liked to give the impression that he had worked everything out beforehand. However, it is far more likely that in the domestic sphere he had no detailed programme and that he dealt with opposition as and when it emerged, on an ad hoc basis. In any case, it was never his way to provoke trouble. But when the government's authority was challenged, his ultimate aims could only be achieved by the defeat of his critics and opponents.

a) The Huguenots

During the first half dozen years of his ministry Richelieu confronted the Habsburgs with one hand tied behind his back. The Huguenots still constituted a state within the state, secure in the political and military guarantees of the Edict of Nantes. As we saw on page 12, Louis XIII's previous attempts to bring his Protestant subjects to heel had ended in stalemate. In 1624 the Huguenots' military organisation was still led by fractious noblemen, and strongholds such as La Rochelle were beyond royal control. The Huguenots themselves were understandably apprehensive, only too open to persuasion by their more hot-headed leaders such as Rohan and his brother Soubise, while Catholics, especially the *dévots,* relished the prospect of a final show-down. There was a general mood of instability and tension.

However Richelieu's attitude was cautiously pragmatic. As Bishop of Luçon he had initially offered the Huguenots 'a relationship based on love'. But he had no sympathy with heresy. He had introduced Capuchins and Oratorians in order to convert Huguenots to Catholicism, and he had demolished a Huguenot *temple* which was too close to his cathedral. On the other hand, he was sceptical about forced conversions, and he was not in favour of gratuitously provoking the Huguenots. Much though the cardinal feared and disliked the military and political threat of the Huguenot movement, he would probably have preferred to let sleeping dogs lie.

But the Huguenots themselves forced the issue. In May 1625 the citizens of La Rochelle joined Sourdis in rebellion, confident that their co-religionists throughout France would join them. Despite the involvement of the king's armies elsewhere (see page 45) this did not happen. The duc de Montmorency in command of a large royal fleet defeated Soubise, and in February 1626 the Rochelais accepted Richelieu's peace terms. These were not generous. The town surrendered its ships, while the king garrisoned Fort-Louis controlling the landward approach and the Ile de Ré cutting off La Rochelle from the sea. Bitterly disillusioned, La Rochelle defied its king again in the following year, in co-operation with Huguenot risings throughout the south of France and an English landing on the Ile de Ré led by the Duke of Buckingham. 'The grievance of grievances', as one of Buckingham's English critics called him, combined complacency with incompetence. After rejecting the French army's offer to negotiate, he failed to capture the Ile de Ré and departed leaving the Rochelais to their fate. With the courage of desperation the townsfolk held out until 28 October 1628; starvation reduced the population from 30,000 to 6,000. Both Louis XIII and Richelieu (in armour, buffcoat and boots) joined the siege. Richelieu designed a barrier of masonry across the harbour mouth. Louis offered to help by wielding a pick-axe much to Richelieu's disapproval - perhaps fearing that he would have to follow his monarch's example. A few weeks later the cardinal triumphantly celebrated mass in the principal church of La Rochelle to mark its return to the Catholic faith.

The following year Richelieu reverted to diplomacy. He was displeased when the royal army sacked Privas in Languedoc with appalling barbarity in May 1629. However, Huguenot resistance now collapsed. On Richelieu's advice Louis issued the Edict of Alès which confirmed the religious clauses of the Edict of Nantes, while rendering the Huguenots militarily harmless. Their armies were disbanded and their fortresses were demolished. But Protestantism survived. Indeed, numbers may even have increased between 1629 and 1661.

While Richelieu would have preferred the Huguenots to have been converted, his chief priorities were achieved, that is to say, the security of the state and the maintenance of royal authority. The political and military problem presented by the Huguenots was now solved, as was shown by the readiness of Rohan to fight for the king against his enemies abroad and the loyalty of the Huguenots for the rest of Louis XIII's reign and during the Fronde.

b) The Nobles

Throughout his ministry Richelieu was challenged by the nobility. Yet, as we saw in the last chapter, he was not anti-noble. The most one can say is that for good reasons he was anti-*some*-nobles! He was an aristocrat himself. He was glad when his relatives married well. He accepted the prevalent view that noblemen constituted an élite whose *raison d'être* was service in the army. He never attacked the nobility's exemption from taxation.

Nevertheless Richelieu was well aware of the threat to political stability and royal authority which aristocrats had posed since 1559. Religious differences and royal minorities had consistently been exploited by the French nobility with the utmost selfishness and cynicism. A typical late-medieval situation prevailed, reminiscent of bastard feudalism in fifteenth century England: a weak crown threatened by overmighty subjects backed by private armies. At the centre of government the intrigues of the nobility often involved princes of the blood, while great magnates dominated their localities by constructing fortresses and exploiting patronage. This nightmare had been compounded by foreign intervention, for the king's subjects had cheerfully invited Englishmen, Dutchmen and above all Spaniards on to French soil in their own interests. All in all, the nobles personified selfish greed. The menace presented to the crown by an over-powerful aristocracy was very apparent to Richelieu.

Nor did it take the nobles long to realise what a menace to their interests Richelieu was. From the day that he took office to the day on which he died his position as chief minister was challenged by the jealousy and hatred of prominent nobles. The cardinal's enemies may or may not have been enemies of the state, but there were certainly plenty of them. This was partly due to Richelieu's abrasive personality, for he had no charm and was too busy to win converts. His own unscrupulous exploitation of patronage inevitably alienated his less successful rivals. Above all his position as chief minister was envied by the ambitious and attacked by those who disagreed with his policies, especially the enhancement of royal authority.

Therefore if Richelieu's blue-blooded enemies wanted to dominate France and monopolise power, in effect they had to procure the removal of the hated chief minister. It is worth remembering when we consider the plots aimed at Richelieu that ultimately the king's credibility was on the line as well, certainly while Richelieu remained Louis' choice as chief minister. The politics of royal authoritarianism versus aristocratic reaction therefore hinged on the outcome of a number of intrigues and plots dedicated to Richelieu's overthrow.

What decided the outcome? The determining factor was the precarious life and the uncertain favour of a moody, unpredictable monarch. In his *Testament Politique* Richelieu wrote with feeling: 'The capacity to be served faithfully is not the least of the qualities of a good king'. But Louis' favour was never to be assumed while his health was no better than Richelieu's. The withdrawal of the king's favour and above all the king's death would have spelt ruin for the cardinal, the green light for revenge so ardently desired by his aristocratic enemies.

Another person who was intensely interested in Louis' health was his brother Gaston, duc d'Orleans. A consistent feature of the plots directed against Richelieu was the involvement of this charming, shallow and disruptive adventurer. Until the birth of the future Louis XIV in September 1638, Gaston was heir to the throne. No wonder that when his nephew the 'miracle child' was born, Gaston insisted on removing the swaddling clothes to check that it really was a boy. Gaston exploited his proximity to the throne - and given the king's ill-health and the frequency of infant mortality it was a highly significant fact - and the opportunities of court patronage to attract to his service a seemingly unending retinue of rash noblemen whom he invariably betrayed to the government when his plots were uncovered. His disloyalty to Louis XIII may even have involved him in schemes to kill the king and certainly led him to flirt with Queen Anne whom he hoped to marry in the happy event of his brother's death.

It was Louis' proposal to marry off Gaston to a suitable heiress, Marie de Montpensier, that provoked the Chalais conspiracy of spring 1626. Gaston intrigued with Henri IV's bastards, the Vendôme brothers, and with a group of nobles, including the comte de Chalais, with connections in England and Holland. How much did Anne of Austria know? This was a worrying question, as the conspirators intended not only the murder of Richelieu but very possibly the deposition of Louis XIII; Gaston would then marry no common or garden heiress but Anne of Austria, the widowed Queen of France. However Richelieu's spies uncovered the conspiracy, arrests were made, and Gaston after contemplating flight decided to turn king's evidence instead. Richelieu conducted the marriage of Gaston, his would-be murderer, and the previously rejected heiress Mme de Montpensier. Chalais was condemned to death as scapegoat for his highly-connected friends who tried to save him by kidnapping the executioner and removing the axe. But all this was in vain. A convict substituted with substituted implements - first a sword (fifteen blows) and then a cooper's mallet (twenty-nine blows). These gruesome details helped to establish Richelieu's reputation for ruthlessness. He and his royal master clearly meant business. Louis gave Richelieu an armed guard and wrote to him in affectionate terms:

> All my affairs, thanks to God, have succeeded well since you were in office. I have every confidence in you, and it is true that I have never found anyone who has served me so much to my taste as you. The Queen Mother makes you a similar promise. Whoever attacks you, you will have me as your second.

The king's duelling metaphor is ironic as Richelieu now attacked this aristocratic privilege. We have noted how precious the knightly code was to the nobility. Some drunken insult, somebody pushed aside in a crowded street, a row over a lady's favours - such were the causes of duels. But the results were far from trivial. Whole families were involved in long-lasting feuds which disrupted law and order even in Paris. An edict of February 1626 therefore banned duelling, threatening participants with banishment and, if fatalities occurred, with death. Such edicts had frequently been issued in the past and were regarded as a joke. On 14 May 1627 Montmorency-Bouteville, a young rip who had twenty-two 'kills' to his credit, staged a duel under the cardinal's window in the Place Royale in broad daylight. One of the six participants was killed. Bouteville was arrested and condemned to death. Louis XIII was bombarded with pleas for clemency, for the young man was a popular member of an ancient house, had a pregnant wife, and had after all been defending the privilege of his order. Louis wavered. But Richelieu reminded his monarch that he would bear the responsibility for future duelling deaths and that if he failed to impose his own law his authority would be severely harmed. So 'Louis the Just' held firm, Bouteville died, and Richelieu's reputation with the nobility sank further.

The turbulent nobility was but one of many problems discussed at an Assembly of Notables (December 1626 - February 1627) - summoned to give the government's critics the impression that they were being consulted. An edict of July 1626 which ordered the destruction of all castles except those on the frontier was confirmed. The offices of Constable and Admiral of France - traditionally the preserves of the ancient nobility - were abolished. These measures were clearly aimed at the nobility. In addition a positive reform programme cutting expenditure and improving the administration of the army and the economy was advocated by Michel de Marillac, the Keeper of the Seals. This reform programme was eventually published in 1629 as the *Code Michaud* (Marillac's nickname was *Michaud)*.

However, Richelieu was uninterested in administrative reform. This was a real weakness especially when his enemies were able to point to the ruinous expense of Richelieu's foreign policy which distracted him from domestic reform. In the next conspiracy therefore not only were important personalities involved - the queen mother, the queen and, of course, Gaston - but genuine policy issues were at stake. The *dévots* were now totally disillusioned with Richelieu. Led by Marillac and his brother Louis, a successful general, and inspired by the influential founder of the Oratorians, Cardinal Bérulle, they attacked Richelieu's costly 'Protestant' foreign policy and blamed him for tolerating Huguenots and ignoring popular demands for lower taxes. Much-needed reforms, for instance those included in the *Code Michaud,* were being sacrificed to Richelieu's ambitions abroad. The self-evident justice of these criticisms made them all the more damaging, especially because Louis XIII was highly religious and much influenced by *dévot* teaching. Nor was he blind to the sufferings of his people.

The crisis came in November 1630. During the summer campaign the king fell ill. He had to leave the army to Richelieu's leadership and submit to the nursing, and therefore the influence, of his mother and his wife. In the autumn the court returned to Paris. Marie de Medici and Marillac were sure that the king was now on their side and that the hated chief minister's fate was sealed. Richelieu was in despair. A final confrontation occurred in the king's presence. Marie shouted like a fishwife at Richelieu. Richelieu collapsed, kissed the hem of Marie's dress, wept, and fled the room. Louis said nothing and left for his hunting-lodge at Versailles. The queen mother and her friends were exultant. But Marie, like many others less close to him, failed to 'read' her own son. Louis summoned Richelieu and rejected his offer of resignation: 'I order you absolutely to remain and continue directing my affairs - that is my irrevocable decision'.

This dramatic crisis was called the Day of Dupes. Ultimately the queen mother and her allies were deceived, although for several days it looked as though Richelieu was the dupe. The crisis reminds us how precarious was his position and how crucial was Louis XIII's support. In retrospect it has an air of finality, for Marie de Medici fled to the Spanish Netherlands never to return. Yet ten days after Louis' crucial decision Richelieu was still grovelling to Marie: 'There is nothing in the world that I would not do to avoid the continuance of your disfavour'. Richelieu apparently could not believe that his ex-patron's hold over him was finished. Perhaps it was a similar basic insecurity which explains Richelieu's gratuitously severe treatment of the Marillac brothers who had once been his friends and colleagues and who were as devoted to France as he was. Michael was imprisoned at Châteaudun where he died two years later. Louis was tried for treason, acquitted, retried in Richelieu's country house, condemned and executed - a shabby business. It was all very well for Richelieu to write: 'In judging crimes against the state it is essential to banish pity'. But his treatment of the Marillacs violated justice, loyalty and common decency. One of Marie de Medici's pamphleteers commented:

> Today it is generally accepted that it is just to imprison anyone because of the slightest wish of a favourite (for all know that these acts do not come from the king). Every suspicion is cause for imprisonment; every imprisonment is authorised by the judges. Every pretext is a crime; every crime is subject to condemnation; every condemnation is for not less than life. Whoever displeases a favourite is put in prison, and whoever is in prison must be executed to justify the act of him who caused him to be imprisoned. Are these maxims of state or of hell?

Patronage dictated the course of the next aristocratic challenge. Henri, duc de Montmorency's family had governed Languedoc for generations. He himself was popular and respected. The province's gentry followed their patron unquestioningly. As it happened the province was unhappy. Richelieu's proposal to introduce *élus* (see page 73) in order to increase tax yields caused much resentment. Montmorency negotiated a compromise, but there was still sufficient unease in Languedoc for Marie de Medici and Gaston to stir up trouble. Furthermore, Montmorency harboured grudges against the chief minister because he had been deprived of the Admiralty and because of the execution of his cousin Bouteville. Therefore, in a fateful moment in July 1632 he threw in his lot with Gaston who marched across France from Lorraine to Languedoc. The provincial nobility followed Montmorency's lead. The combined rebel army was defeated in a pitched battle by the king's general Schomberg at Castelnaudary. Montmorency fought with desperate courage; having failed to find death on the battlefield, he was taken prisoner. Once again the king was besieged with appeals for mercy, but once again he ruled that the traitor must die. Montmorency was entitled to trial by his peers. But Richelieu doubted whether the duc's peers would get it right, so Montmorency was condemned by the *Parlement* of Toulouse - in his own province. He died bravely and bequeathed his best pictures to Richelieu.

Louis XIII stood by his chief minister against Montmorency but he wobbled horrifyingly in the last confrontation with the aristocracy, the Cinq Mars affair. The king needed love and sympathy but failed to attract them from his wife. So he bestowed his affection on a number of male and female favourites, some of whom interfered in politics. For example, the saintly Mme de La Fayette who became a nun and yet continued to converse with the king through a grille when he visited her convent, criticised France's anti-Habsburg foreign policy. Richelieu decided to put a stop to this nonsense by 'planting' a reliably stupid and non-political favourite to replace the nun. He thought that he had found just the person in Henri Coiffier de Ruzé, marquis de Cinq-Mars - a beautiful and brainless nineteen-year-old. At first the plan seemed a success. The susceptible king was infatuated with Cinq-Mars whom he loaded with riches and honours, making him *Grand Ecuyer de France* (Master of the Horse). However, events proved that Richelieu had been too clever. For 'Monsieu le Grand', as everyone called Cinq-Mars, soon became insufferably conceited. He despised his royal friend, torturing the pathetic and vulnerable prude with salacious accounts of his own affairs with court ladies and was rude to Richelieu when taken to task for his arrogance.

In these distressing circumstances on cue as ever, Gaston recruited Cinq-Mars for his latest plot to assassinate Richelieu and end the war. The fact that many noblemen applauded both objectives brought in a number of high-ranking recruits such as the duc de Bouillon, commander of the garrison at Sedan. The conspirators approached Olivares, Richelieu's Spanish opposite number, and in March 1642 a treaty was signed by which France would abandon her Protestant allies.

Richelieu however was tipped off by an unlikely informant. A few months before the Cinq Mars conspiracy, after being subjected to humiliating, third-degree interrogation by her husband and his chief minister, Anne of Austria had confessed to treasonable correspondence with her brother, the Cardinal Infante. Terrified that she would be punished by losing custody of her sons she was pathetically anxious to appease her persecutors. So she now told Richelieu all she knew. But Richelieu still hesitated to confront Louis, so infatuated was the king with 'Monsieu le Grand'.

A ghastly charade was played out during the early summer as the court moved south to the siege of Perpignan on the Spanish frontier. Both the king and his chief minister were mortally ill. Indeed Richelieu was in such pain that he could not get up from the huge litter on which he travelled; every night walls had to be holed so that he could be carried into the house where he was to sleep. By contrast Cinq-Mars personified youthful good health. But even though he was dying, Richelieu was still capable of trapping the plotters so conclusively that not even the love-sick Louis could deny the evidence. At Lyons Richelieu presented the facts to the king. Devastated, Louis ordered the conspirators' arrest. Gaston told all. Cinq-Mars was tried and condemned by the ever dependable Chancellor, Seguier. Richelieu wanted Cinq-Mars tortured after his trial but was overruled by the judges. On 12 September 1642 the pathetic young man was executed before a huge crowd who were treated to another botched job. With a weary sense of achievement Richelieu remarked: 'Perpignan is in the king's hands, and Monsieu le Grand is in the next world'. Louis had backed his chief minister but ceased to address him affectionately or to ask after his health. He was too heart-broken.

When death overtook the great cardinal in December, it cannot be said that the problem of the nobility had been solved. True, Richelieu had survived all attempts to remove him from power. But this achievement was at best a holding operation. He had not even eradicated duelling - as he admitted in his *Testament Politique*. Indeed aristocratic turbulence remained an endemic feature of French politics. This threat to good order and social stability was exacerbated by the wars in which France became involved. For the only way in which French governments knew how to raise and supply armies was virtually to hand them over to their blue-blooded commanders. What was to prevent a general leading his troops against the crown? Richelieu's solution whenever possible was to appoint his own relations to sensitive commands. We have seen his dependence on royal favour; add patronage and nepotism, and you have the cardinal's 'system'. He also needed luck. After the rebel comte de Soissons had defeated a royal army, he raised the visor of his helmet with a pistol - and blew his own brains out. But self-destruction did not always come to the rescue of French governments. As soon as Richelieu was dead, the king allowed the cardinal's enemies to return home. The stage was set for the Fronde, when it would become apparent how little Richelieu had achieved. His own survival against aristocratic plots was remarkable. But the French nobility had neither been reconciled nor dragooned into accepting royal supremacy and its corollary, their own political emasculation. That task would eventually be accomplished by Louis XIV who was neither as clever as Richelieu nor as remorseless as Louis XIII - but who possessed qualities which both men lacked: subtlety and charm.

c) The *Parlements*

Royal authority clashed with the sovereign courts, so called because they traced their origins back to the medieval *curia regis* (the king's council). These courts included the *Cours des Aides* which settled taxation disputes and the *Chambres des Comptes* which registered and audited taxes. However, the most influential sovereign courts were the *Parlements* which claimed the right to register royal edicts after scrutinising and criticising them. During the past two centuries provincial *Parlements* had been created at Toulouse, Grenoble, Bordeaux, Dijon, Rouen, Aix-en-Provence and Rennes. But the *Parlement de Paris* was much the most prestigious and influential of the sovereign courts. Although it could not claim to represent the whole realm, the failure of the Estates General in 1614-15 (see pages 8-10) to behave responsibly had enhanced the prestige of the *Parlement de Paris*.

During Richelieu's period of office the government made provocative use of the *lit de justice* (literally 'bed of justice') which enabled a royal edict to be imposed without the *Parlements'* approval. Equally resented was the crown's use of *commissaires* (special representatives) who overruled the sovereign courts, hi-jacking politically sensitive cases by the authority of the royal council. Similarly the king's council imposed taxes and created new offices without consulting the sovereign courts in order to finance the cardinal's increasingly expensive foreign policy. There was ample material here for conflict.

Richelieu's dispensation of arbitrary justice became notorious. Hand-picked judges 'tried' Marillac, Montmorency and Cinq-Mars. The *Chambre de l'Arsenal* was a special court set up by Richelieu to punish political offenders. Its victims were arrested and executed by night. The *Parlement de Paris* refused this court official registration when it was created in 1631, but eventually gave way in January 1632. This climb-down occurred after a deputation of parlementaires journeyed to Metz to be lectured by their king: 'You are here only to judge master Peter and master John, and I intend to keep you in your place; if you continue your machinations, I will cut your nails to the quick'. Louis was even more forthright when the *Parlement* of Bordeaux protested against the judicial activities of Richelieu's high-handed *intendants;* Louis interrupted the president in full flow by pulling his sleeve and shouting,

'To your knees, little man, before your master'.

However Louis XIII's and Richelieu's apparently tyrannical treatment of the sovereign courts is only half the story. In actual practice the government regularly listened to criticism and made concessions, for instance with regard to taxes and the creation of new offices. Louis XIII, who it must be stressed was always the final arbiter of his government's policies, overruled the rights of his subjects only when in his judgement the welfare of the state demanded it. He never questioned the existence of those rights or imposed burdens which the the public good did not require. Thus the king's chancellor justified the creation of new offices to the *Parlement de Paris:*

> The king was well aware of the great expenses with which the people of his kingdom were burdened; he regretted that they had been imposed and that they were continuing; but the well-being of the state and the preservation of his kingdom had forced him to act thus, and of the mildest remedies available he had been advised to create new offices, which would not seriously strain his finances or seriously trouble the people.

Similarly Louis XIII never forgot that the sovereign courts - which in origin were his courts - could be a source of strength to the crown. The *Parlement de Paris* had supported Henri IV in the final stages of the religious wars, had registered the Edict of Nantes and had defended the crown's control of the French church against the papacy. It had boosted Marie de Medici's authority when she became regent after Henri IV's murder. And it was to the *Parlement de Paris* that Louis turned before his death so as to limit Anne of Austria's power as regent by requiring her to accept Gaston and Condé as colleagues.

The government's policy towards the sovereign courts was therefore ambivalent. On the one hand, Louis XIII and Richelieu dealt with opposition in a high-handed way. On the other hand, they showed themselves aware that the magistrates who staffed the courts and the crown had crucial interests in common. It would be nonsense to suggest that the rights of the sovereign courts were systematically and deliberately repressed in a radical drive towards absolutism.

Two points must be stressed. The first is that to an increasing extent the government's combination of authoritarianism and concession achieved its purpose. The combination of a formidable monarch, a resourceful chief minister and a flexible approach realistically geared to the exceptional circumstances of the times defeated would-be protestors and critics. The necessary measures to fund the mounting costs of the government's foreign policy and silence the voices of discontent were adopted. The second is that these more aggressive royal policies caused increasing indignation and outrage which seethed beneath the surface and would create serious problems in the long term.

When different circumstances prevailed, for example in Paris and in Bordeaux between 1648 and 1653, Louis' and Richelieu's heirs paid the price for the crown's high-handed actions.

5 The Economy and Government Finance

Given that challenges to royal authority were more or less contained, it should have been relatively easy to raise the taxation with which to fight France's foreign enemies. But this did not prove to be the case, for the necessary prosperity which could support high taxation did not exist. A long coastline, rich soil and a mild climate should have made France wealthy. Instead dire poverty affected the majority of French people. Compared to contemporary Holland and Britain, trade languished and industry stagnated. Above all French agriculture failed to emerge from its late-medieval backwardness.

There were two reasons for this depressing state of affairs. First, the government's positive steps to improve the economy were misconceived and probably did more harm than good. The second was the crown's insatiable need for money. Taxes, which were unfairly imposed and inefficiently collected, were so heavy that they inevitably damaged the economy, hitting those who could least afford to pay.

a) Richelieu's Economic Policies

Ironically Richelieu was more interested, better informed and had wider-ranging ideas than most of his contemporaries. He genuinely wished to improve trade and industry, and was aware that widespread poverty was a national disaster. In his constructive approach to economic affairs he anticipated Colbert, Louis XIV's chief minister; 'Colbert will now tell us what Cardinal Richelieu would have done', Louis XIV would remark sardonically in council meetings. Like Colbert Richelieu admired and envied Dutch economic efficiency. Unfortunately, however, Richelieu failed to appreciate how best his government could help to develop the French economy, and what the priorities should be.

Perhaps Richelieu's most intelligent and beneficial idea was to found the French navy. He thereby protected and encouraged trade, stimulated the ship-building industry and created thousands of jobs. In 1626 he appointed himself Grand Master and Superintendent General of Commerce and Navigation after abolishing the post of Admiral of France. When someone objected that only the governor of Brittany was allowed to supervise shipping, Richelieu made himself governor of Brittany. French merchants were being bullied by the Spaniards and the British, and outsold by the Dutch. In the Mediterranean, pirates from north Africa not only captured French ships and enslaved their crews but even raided Toulon and Marseille. Richelieu established a garrison at Toulon, dockyards at Brest - which he founded - and re-established La Rochelle. In 1626 France had an admiral but no navy. Ten years later 46 ocean-going French warships operated from the Atlantic ports, by 1642 there were 63, while a fleet of 22 galleys operated in the Mediterranean, manned by criminals arrested by Richelieu's *intendants*. Richelieu granted a pension to the inventor of a submarine. French warships helped to reduce the Huguenot stronghold of La Rochelle and Henri de Sourdis, Archbishop of Bordeaux, (Richelieu's cousin) led the Atlantic fleet to victory over the Spaniards.

This achievement was all the more creditable given that there was little French maritime experience or tradition which Richelieu could exploit. England, Spain and Holland by contrast had well-established seafaring traditions and centuries of experience. If France had a naval tradition, it was piracy, and indeed French piracy was often the most effective weapon against France's enemies. The navy was to go through troubled times after Richelieu's death, though it gave a creditable account of itself against the British and the Dutch in Louis XIV's reign. But this would have been unthinkable without the foundations which Richelieu laid. It was appropriate that France's two largest twentieth century battleships should be named *Jean Bart* (one of Louis XIV's pirates) and *Richelieu*.

Equally enterprising though less successful was Richelieu's colonial policy. He began by founding trading companies such as the *compagnie de la Nacelle de Saint Pierre Fleur-delysée* which was supposed to inaugurate a great trans-oceanic empire. In 1626 New France was founded covering present-day Nova Scotia where a handful of Frenchmen lived precariously on fishing and the fur trade, constantly under attack from Red Indians, Englishmen, wild beasts and the weather. Richelieu did his best to support New France and also the French settlement which Samuel Champlain had founded at Quebec in 1608. But French colonists were outfought and outfished by the English, and there were only 200 colonists when Richelieu died. *Dévot* influence ensured the maximum emphasis on the conversion of the Indians to the Catholic faith and the total exclusion of Huguenots, who might well have made an effective contribution with their austere life style and commercial experience. But dogma triumphed over common sense. A convent, a girls' school and a school for young Indians were no substitute for traders. Ironically French colonisation was more successful in the Caribbean where Richelieu showed less interest. However, he became a member of the *Compagnie des Iles d'Amérique* and contributed a ship. This company made a profit by manufacturing sugar and transporting slaves. Over 7,000 French colonists were established on St Kitts, Guadeloupe and Martinique; the guiding light of this highly realistic project was the Breton merchant Nicholas Fouquet whom we shall meet again. Richelieu also established colonies of French merchants in the Baltic; no French ships passed through the Sound between Denmark and Sweden in 1628, 20 in 1630 and 72 in 1631.

Richelieu was well aware that if French trade was to prosper, her merchants must have something to sell; yet here too his achievement was slender. He rightly deplored France's unproductivity and in particular the backwardness of her industry. During Louis XIII's reign France's mines and factories achieved less than a third of England's production - and England's population was probably a third of France's. Richelieu made the situation worse by stifling French production with government regulations. No master craftsman was allowed to produce without a permit. The shop floor was dominated by guilds all of which had to be registered with the government. Royal inspectors interfered in the production of iron and beer. Ostensibly the objective was to raise standards. In truth the goal was to raise money for Richelieu's foreign policy. The results were deplorable, and it is significant that the Norman uprising of 1639 began with the lynching of a textiles inspector in Rouen. The only field in which Richelieu intervened effectively was the luxury market. He encouraged the silk manufacturers of Tours, while carpets were produced at the Louvre, glass in Picardy and mirrors in Paris. Otherwise it is a story of grandiose schemes but only modest achievements.

Not all of Richelieu's ideas were unrealistic or absurd. He improved the postal service, introduced stage-coaches and completed the Briare canal which Henri IV had begun. He tried to prevent bullion leaving the country by taxing foreign luxury goods and encouraging French exports - a policy which historians now reckon had more to be said for it than used to be supposed. He did his best to combat prejudices against trade; under his influence the *Code Michau* of 1629 abolished the punishing of noblemen who traded, though unfortunately aristocrats were slow to respond to this opportunity. Similarly, after opposing the importing of luxuries from the Levant because they drained France of precious metals, Richelieu changed his approach, appreciating that however desirable the husbanding of French coinage the Levant trade gave employment to thousands, stimulated ship-building and raised revenue for the crown:

> I admit that I was long mistaken about the trade of the Provenceaux with the Levant. I believed along with many others that it was damaging to the state, sharing the common view that it drained the kingdom of money simply in order to import inessential luxuries. But, after acquiring a precise knowledge of that unpopular trade, I have changed my mind for reasons that are so well grounded that anyone who troubles to find them out will see that I am right. *(Testament Politique)*

But Richelieu's ultimate priorities conflicted with France's economic welfare. Everything was sacrificed to the war against the Habsburgs. As we shall see in the next section the horrendous cost of the war was met by soaring taxation. This severely damaged French industry and trade because most people could only afford the barest essentials, nor had the government any spare cash which could be profitably invested. War drove merchant ships off the sea; for example the promising Baltic trade had disappeared completely by 1633. Above all, French agriculture languished as more and more peasants were ruined by the billeting of troops and by the demands of the taxman. However, the failure to support and modernise French agriculture which remained a late-medieval phenomenon until the nineteenth century (and beyond?) cannot wholly be blamed on governments. It reflected the prejudices of the French upper classes who preferred to invest in the purchase of office or in government bonds, contrasting vividly with their estate-managing English contemporaries. There is no evidence that Richelieu appreciated the seriousness of this problem or the possibility of affecting improvements in, say, the growth of cereals, the breeding of cattle or the production of wine. His eyes were fixed on the battlefields of Europe rather than the harvest fields of France.

b) Taxation and Popular Protest

> I fully admit my ignorance of financial matters and I realise that you are so well-versed in the subject that the only advice I can give you is to make use of those whom you find most useful to the king's service, and to rest assured that I will second you in every way I can. (Richelieu to Bullion, 1635)

These oft-quoted words show Richelieu at his most disingenuous. He may not have been a financial wizard, but he knew more about finance than virtually anyone else at the court of Louis XIII. He was fully capable of appreciating the likely consequences of his expensive foreign policy which would somehow have to be paid for. He was glad to leave decisions about how this money was to be raised to subordinates such as Bullion who could then be blamed for the suffering caused. But there is no excuse for historians to be fooled. Whether the objectives of Richelieu's foreign policy were the right ones for France and whether those objectives could have been achieved at less cost, are questions which will be tackled in the conclusion to this chapter. Our immediate concerns are the methods by which taxes were raised to pay for the wars and the impact of these measures on the internal development of France. As chief minister Richelieu was ultimately responsible for both methods and impact.

To be fair, it was not easy to find the necessary cash. France's annual military expenditure more than doubled, from 16 million to 38 million livres, between 1624 and 1642, while in addition considerable subsidies were paid to France's allies. The problems of finding the money were compounded by disruption of trade caused by war, foreign invasions and billeting of troops.

In theory this should not have presented insuperable difficulties, for on paper the king's revenue in 1636 came to 108 million livres. There were three sources of this revenue: direct revenue (taxation of individuals), indirect revenue (tax paid on the purchase of commodities or during the course of trading) and extraordinary revenues (money raised from the sale of government bonds and offices, and borrowings from money-lenders). In practice, however, the king was lucky if he received half the money that was his due.

The main source of direct revenue was the *taille* of which there were two kinds: the *taille réelle,* a land tax which was voted by the estates in the *pays d'état,* and the *taille personnelle* which was a poll tax levied in the rest of France. It was a notorious fact that the *pays d'état* (Languedoc, Provence, Dauphiné, Burgundy, Brittany, and Normandy) were scandalously undertaxed; although together they constituted a third of France, they paid one tenth of the total taxes of the country. However, when historians talk about the *taille* it is usually the *taille personnelle* which they mean. This tax was paid by most of the third estate in the *pays d'élection* - the clergy, the nobility, office-holders and privileged localities such as the city of Paris were exempt - where no legal opposition to taxation was possible. Its total amount was fixed annually by the king's council of finance which then informed the *trésoriers* who were the officials in charge of fiscal areas known as *généralités.* They in their turn allocated amounts to local officials called *élus* who were responsible for *élections* which were divided into parishes. In theory all these officials were supposed to discuss with their subordinates how much each area could be expected to contribute, and to check the justice of the assessments by personal inspection.

In practice the collection of the *taille* was a perpetual headache to the government. In times of peace and prosperity it could be administered satisfactorily even by dishonest and incompetent officials. Unfortunately the increasing demands of the government coincided in the 1630s with a European recession, a series of poor harvests and persistent outbreaks of plague. In these conditions tax officials who, it should be remembered, had bought their positions and expected to make a profit, became increasingly corrupt, violent and ineffectual. The peasants hated the tax which was unevenly assessed and inconsistently collected; if the local official was a friend of yours, you were less likely to be hard hit. Backlogs of unpaid *taille* led to confiscations of property and imprisonment of officials. By the late 1630s troops were used in order to collect *taille. Fusiliers pour les tailles,* as they were called, were light cavalry who accompanied tax-collectors on their rounds. They drove unco-operative peasants from their homes, helped themselves to moveable property, were generally encouraged to behave badly and had to be paid for by the localities where they were billeted. This use of troops to extract money justifies the term 'fiscal terrorism'. Ultimately it was counter-productive, causing ever-increasing bitterness and non-co-operation. In 1634 Richelieu had a better idea. *Intendants* were appointed initially to inspect the activities of tax officials, then to fix assessments and finally to replace the officials as tax-collectors. However, even they could not prevent the yield from the *taille* falling seriously into arrears.

The situation with regard to indirect taxation became equally unsatisfactory. Long before Richelieu's day indirect taxes had been privatised, that is to say farmed out to contractors called *traitants* (from *traité* meaning an agreement). The contactors promised to produce for the government an agreed amount in return for the right to extract as much money as possible from the levying of the tax. It was clearly an imperfect system which encouraged graft and extortion. The most hated of all indirect taxes was the *gabelle* - the salt-tax. Salt was a necessity for everyone in an age when beasts were killed off in the autumn and their carcasses salted to last through the winter. The collectors of this tax, the *gabelleurs,* were often the targets of violent resentment, their corruption being notorious. In his *Testament* Richelieu admitted that of 19 million livres collected annually by the *gabelleurs* only 5 million normally reached the treasury. As war restricted both trade and consumption, the yield from indirect taxes declined, forcing the government to look elsewhere.

To an ever-increasing extent Richelieu and his ministers resorted to extraordinary revenues. More and more *rentes* (government bonds) were put on the market (11 million livres worth in February 1634), to be purchased by *rentiers* for cash in return for a guaranteed income in the future; in other words the future was mortgaged for the sake of the present. More and more offices were created to be sold to the highest bidder; again, cash down, the taxpayer will pick up the bill in future years. Huge sums of money were borrowed, usually at 20 per cent interest, with the tax revenues for future years as security. By 1640 the government was paying 48.8 million livres a year to office-holders and *rentiers,* loans totalling 37.6 million livres had been negotiated and the revenues for the next two years were mortgaged to financiers. In other words the state was heading for bankruptcy.

One word - desperation - sums up the impact of these taxation policies on the life-styles of individual French people. The proof is that despair drove millions to armed revolt. Historians have claimed that during the half century from 1625 to 1675 spontaneous uprisings against harsh social and economic conditions became almost a way of life in the French countryside. Many of these revolts were local affairs involving only a few villages, quickly and no doubt brutally suppressed and virtually unrecorded. However, three major rebellions can be identified: in Quercy (1626), the *Croquants* (the starving) in the south-west (1636-7), and the *Nu-pieds* (the bare-footed) in Normandy

(1639). The Russian historian B.F. Porchnev has applied a Marxist explanation of these uprisings, seeing here a class protest by exploited peasants and artisans against parasitic merchants and landlords. Most historians reject Porchnev's interpretation as simplistic and misleading. While there certainly was an element of envy and hatred of the privileged (how could there not be?) the over-riding impression is of whole districts rising up against central governmental interference in general and the royal tax-collectors in particular. The *Croquants* were led by a nobleman, La Mothe la Forêt, who imposed military organisation and discipline. Often the nobility and office-holders would look the other way when tax-collectors were lynched and the *gabelleurs'* warehouses plundered. Lower Normandy defied royal authority for several months in 1639 after a suspicious-looking stranger had been lynched in Avranches for allegedly planning the introduction of the *gabelle.* The rebels called themselves 'the army of suffering', a revealing title. As we shall see in chapter 4, hostility towards high taxation was behind the Fronde rebellions (1648-53) which Richelieu's successors had to face.

c) An Achievement of Sorts?

Richelieu's management of the French economy is a depressing story. He ignored agriculture, which remained backward and inefficient. About trade and industry he had some promising ideas, but they were not followed through. As for finance and taxation, a bad system was made worse; inefficient machinery was driven to the point of disintegration in a desperate attempt to find the money. When one recalls that all this time Richelieu was making his own fortune, one would expect historians to deliver a harsh verdict on his economic record.

Certainly, the ministers who were responsible to Richelieu for the management of the economy have had a bad press. Richard Bonney thinks that the best of a poor bunch was d'Effiat who was finance minister from 1626 until his death in 1632. D'Effiat, Bonney reckons, was fairly honest and reasonably competent, introducing much-needed reforms and keeping expenditure down to an average of 42 million livres a year. But d'Effiat was fortunate to be in charge of finance before the costs of war escalated. His unlucky successor Claude de Bullion (not an entirely appropriate name) according to Bonney achieved the worst of all worlds, failing to find enough money while at the same time bankrupting the crown and ruining the national economy; 'he operated an illogical and unpopular system which penalised the many for the few'. Perhaps the one thing Bullion got right was to devalue the livre in 1636; a magnificent new coin the *Louis d'or* was minted, French exports became more competitive, the real value of France's subsidies to her allies was reduced and the government made a profit of 2 million livres. Otherwise Bullion had no constructive ideas except to place the government in the hands of financiers who were prepared to lend money on terms advantageous to themselves. When Bullion died in 1640 he had to be buried in secret to avoid public demonstrations of joy. His successor Bouthillier was even worse; Louis XIII pointed out that he was too weak a character ever to say 'No' to Richelieu's requests for cash.

Yet astonishingly Richelieu has escaped blame. 'I do not understand finance' has been accepted as a valid excuse. This is too kind, for after all he was in charge of the government. A fairer verdict would be that Richelieu inherited a bad system which he had neither the time nor the inclination to improve. All that he cared about was getting the money to finance his wars. So taxation remained a corrupt and inefficient shambles. Significantly all treasury accounts were burnt after audit - supposedly to minimise *'une confusion horrible'* (a contemporary description) but in reality to save officials from the prosecution which they deserved. In the 1660s Colbert was to demonstrate the feasibility of tax reform. To argue that Richelieu and his ministers had no alternatives will not do. The truth is that Richelieu looked the other way while tax-payers were fleeced.

6 Richelieu's Absolutism

We have now established that Richelieu's policies were implemented at a high price in terms of human suffering and the nation's resources. As we have seen, and shall see further in the next section, plenty of well-informed and intelligent people rejected Richelieu's priorities and criticised his methods. Personally he was envied and hated with good reason. During the last seven years of his tenure of power (1635-42) France's entry into the Thirty Years War exacerbated the problems which he had caused. No wonder that bonfires were lit when he died. One historian has suggested that Richelieu's greatest achievement was to stay in power for eighteen years. There is some merit in this claim, but it is probably fairer to argue that the considerable success with which he obtained the money to finance his foreign policy - despite the cost in human and economic terms, despite opposition and unpopularity - was an even more impressive achievement. How did he manage it? Is 'absolutism' the answer?

One thing we can definitely say is that the old-fashioned version of Richelieu's absolutism is wrong - that with effortless superiority he outmanoeuvred his opponents in setting up an anticipation of the modern police state. On the contrary, Richelieu retained power and achieved his results with the utmost difficulty and as a result of desperate struggles which could have gone either way. Nothing could be further from the ice-cold political genius of legend than the dying neurotic who battled against Cinq-Mars for his political survival.

Another myth that should be disposed of is that Louis XIII was a figurehead while the great cardinal exercised real power. Some historians have corrected this impression by referring to a 'duo-cephalic' monarchy. But even this is wrong. There were not two heads, there was one. From first to last Richelieu was the king's chief minister and no more; 'I was zero which means something only when there are numbers in front of it', Richelieu remarked in retrospect. Louis XIII's biographer Lloyd Moote argues that the king had strong ideas of his own which had to be obeyed. For example, the decisions in favour of war were Louis', as was the refusal of mercy to condemned conspirators. It has indeed been suggested that Louis' essential cruelty emerges in both these policies; he enjoyed warfare and whereas his father had been Henri the Merciful, he was Louis the Just who played it by the book with relish, sending traitors to the death which they so richly deserved.

Not only was Louis the boss, he was also harsh and unpredictable. Even Richelieu handled him with kid gloves, employing one of his 'creatures' to stay close to the king, report on his moods and pick the right moment to present requests or suggestions. Richelieu never made Concini's and Luyenes' mistake of allowing the king to think that he was being ignored, for Louis was quick to complain to Richelieu if his wishes were defied:

> I gave all the orders for the levying of the six regiments and also for the two new ones and for the whole cavalry. I am writing to you in anger after a commissioner named Renart cut down all the old regiments by 400 men ... all done under the orders of Monsieur de Bullion without having spoken to me about it. It is indeed strange that they give such orders without my knowing it.

On such occasions ministers relied on Richelieu to protect them. Here is Claude de Bouthillier writing anxiously to his patron:

> I saw by a letter of Monsieu de Noyers to Monsieu the Chancellor that the king was displeased that we created the office of provosts generals for the province in council without talking about it to His Majesty. His Eminence will remember, if it please him, that I gave myself the honour of talking to him about it.

This letter illustrates a vitally important reason for Richelieu's survival as chief minister. He fully appreciated that his predecessors had been undermined by their own colleagues, as previous ministries had always contained rival factions. Indeed Louis XIII had welcomed the opportunity of playing groups of ministers off against each other. Richelieu was determined to counteract this. He therefore built up a team of colleagues consisting wholly of his own clients - or creatures. Naturally he could not achieve this overnight; one is reminded of Mussolini taking six years to eliminate unsympathetic colleagues after he had come to power. The Day of Dupes enabled Richelieu finally to remove his last rivals (see page 59).

Thereafter the most important ministers were all Richelieu's clients, totally loyal to their patron and unquestioning in their obedience. Thus when Richelieu rebuked Bullion for 'not taking up the king's affairs with the same passion and ardour that you demonstrate in your own', Bullion could only mutter under his breath about Richelieu's 'expenses'. Typical of Richelieu's ministers was Sublet de Noyers, secretary of state for war - a self-effacing, conscientious little man with a gift for organisation; although his attempts at creating order out of chaos have been exaggerated, he has some claim to be the creator of the French armies of the future. Or there were the Bouthilliers, father and son, responsible for foreign affairs and finance; family friends of Richelieu, they were totally subservient, incapable both of initiative and disloyalty. Readers will recall Louis XIII's concern that the elder Bouthillier lacked the courage to say 'No' (see page 71). The younger Bouthillier who bought himself the estate and title of Chavigny was known as 'Monsieu le Jeune' - and with good reason since he was only twenty-four when appointed secretary of state for foreign affairs. 'Could he be Richelieu's son?' was the court's reaction. But there was no need for such speculation. Chavigny was an ideal appointment from Richelieu's point of view. Ambitious, urbane, intelligent but weak, Chavigny performed his official duties meticulously and unofficially used his charm to smooth relations between his patron the cardinal and both Louis and Gaston.

Richelieu promoted many of his own relatives. His brother, the eccentric monk, became Archbishop of Lyon; his cousin, de Sourdis, became Archbishop of Bordeaux and, as we have seen, a successful admiral; another cousin, La Meilleraye, administered the navy; his uncle became an *intendant;* and his nephew, de Brézé, negotiated with the King of Sweden. Richelieu detached Condé from his disruptive friends, married his own niece to Condé's son, the duc d'Enghien, and promoted his new son-in-law to an army command in which he was brilliantly successful. Richelieu would have agreed with Admiral Fisher, the creator of the modern British navy, that 'nepotism is the secret of efficiency'. These men, Richelieu's clients and relatives, were his eyes and ears, wholly reliable and dependent on their patron. Under his protection they married well, enriched themselves and governed France. After Richelieu's death, they were disgraced. But while he lived, together they made a formidable team.

'They governed France' - but how? Were there radical institutional and administrative developments? We have already noted the government's campaign against the sovereign courts. Comparable victories were achieved in the 1630s when Richelieu persuaded Dauphiné, Burgundy and Provence to trade their status as *pays d'états* in return for tax concessions, thus enabling government officials to administer these provinces without the intervention of the local estates.

However Richelieu was too realistic to attempt similar arrangements with such fiercely independent provinces as Languedoc and Brittany. He was similarly realistic in his relations with provincial governors. Sometimes a high-handed approach was appropriate, as in the replacement of Montmorency after the failure of his revolt in Languedoc or Richelieu's successful takeover in Brittany. However, co-operation rather than confrontation was the norm with the great aristocrats who governed the provinces. This especially applies to the introduction of *intendants* - first to supervise tax officials such as *trésoriers* and *élus,* then by 1642 actually to take over the collection of taxes. It used to be thought that the *intendants* represented a deliberate challenge to provincial governors. However, recent research has shown that more often governors were glad of the *intendant's* support. 'No fundamental conflict of social or political interests developed between them' (R.R.Harding).

Be that as it may, the *intendant* was the ideal instrument in the crises of the 1630s and 1640s. Richard Bonney has written, 'War, above all the fiscal demands of war, was to prove the decisive factor in the establishment of the *intendants'*. Between 1630 and 1648 150 were appointed, many of them serving with the armies and dealing with discipline, billeting, provisions and pay. They served for three years only, they did not purchase their posts and therefore could be dismissed. They were flexible, effective and obedient. Much of Richelieu's success can be attributed to the *intendants.* Not only did they raise money, but they were real *agents de combat* when it was necessary to counter opposition. While major revolts were suppressed by royal armies and chancellor Seguier's judicial repression as in Normandy (1639), the *intendants* dealt with minor opposition. In July 1629 La Thuillerie, the *intendant* in Poitou, levied two companies of cavalry to put down protests against taxation. Foullé mopped up in Quercy in August 1637, again sending in troops where the *taille* had not been paid and prosecuting disruptive peasants. Laffemas, *intendant* in Champagne, wrote to Seguier in March 1633:

> I will not bore you with affairs on this occasion except to tell you that I have issued decrees for the arrest of 34 gentlemen and others who have levied troops against the king and I am ready to issue decrees against eight more, who cause much trouble in the province. Since most of them have had to be sentenced in their absence, I would be very grateful if you would let me know what the king wants to be done with their houses. The people expect to see them made an example to deter others from following suit.

Administrative innovations went hand in hand with forward-looking attempts to harness art and literature in the government's service. As we have seen, Richelieu was a discerning patron of architects and painters, whom he used both to glorify himself and the state. Prominently displayed at his chateau at Richelieu were portraits of the king and queen and paintings of victories achieved during the reign. Paris was embellished with new squares and palaces glorifying Louis XIII. Richelieu built a new chapel for the Sorbonne which was to be both his own mausoleum and a tribute to French culture. In 1634 the *Académie Française* was founded to preserve and improve the beauty of the French language. The use to which the *Académie* could be put is illustrated by Richelieu's row with Pierre Corneille, the greatest dramatist of the age. Corneille's play *Le Cid* produced in 1637 offended Richelieu for three reasons: the hero was a Spaniard, he fought duels, and he represented the aristocratic tradition of violence for the sake of family honour which Richelieu was trying to outlaw. This is how Corneille's hero justifies himself:

> Your father's action, irreparable,
> Disgraced my father, covering me with shame.
> A man of honour's outraged by a slap;
> I shared in the affront, sought out the Count,
> And I avenged my father and my name.
> I'd do it, were it to be done, again.

This glorification of the duel outraged Richelieu, so he asked the *Académie* to condemn the play. The *Académie's* first response was not hostile enough, so Richelieu told it to think again. As is often the way with censorship, the more the play was condemned, the more popular it became. But Corneille dedicated his next work to the cardinal.

Richelieu's most overt attempt to influence and direct public opinion was the *Gazette,* founded in February 1635. This was a sophisticated attempt to present the government's achievements in a favourable light. Glowing references to the king and his chief minister were intermingled with damaging and unfair attacks on the government's critics. Minor victories were given prominence and details damaging to France's image were suppressed. Richelieu himself wrote ghosted articles and corrected the magazine's proofs. At four sous the *Gazette* was too expensive for most breakfast tables, but it came out every Saturday, was displayed at street corners and was widely read.

Do Richelieu's remarkable and enterprising innovations justify the claim that he was 'the founder of French absolutism'? The answer to this question must depend to a great extent on what one means by 'absolutism'. As we have seen, some historians deny that the term can usefully be employed at all in the context of seventeenth century politics. If, however, we accept that absolute rule meant the absence of constitutional and legal checks and as a consequence the exercise of unfettered royal power, did the French monarchy during Richelieu's chief ministry make significant progress in this direction?

The answer has to be 'Yes'. It cannot be questioned that Richelieu radically altered the political landscape of seventeenth-century France in breaking down opposition to the Crown. For by defending his own position and his own policies he was ultimately defending the monarch who employed him. Richelieu's *intendants* ensured that the king's writ ran where it had never run before. In order to raise unprecedented revenue for his foreign policy, Richelieu significantly developed the coercive power of the state. Richelieu's intelligent exploitation of propaganda on behalf of his royal master justified this process, demonstrating that the king represented and defended the state's true interests.

On the other hand, whether Richelieu was really the founder of so-called absolute monarchy is another matter. For without doubt the cardinal built on the achievements of his predecessors. Henri IV was fond of saying 'I mean to be obeyed', and during his brief reign he did much to restore the monarchy's credibility. Even Marie de Medici is now believed to have defended the authority and independence of the crown. Furthermore we have seen how in a very real sense Richelieu was but the minion of Louis XIII who must ultimately take the credit for the achievements of his reign. Again, Richelieu's alleged 'foundations' were proved in subsequent years to be decidedly shaky given the immense problems which he bequeathed to his successors. Did he really found anything?

When we examine these issues, others, perhaps more interesting, arise. The suffering which Richelieu caused the French people was immense. Due to his policies the gap between privileged and unprivileged, between rich and poor, widened. When the cardinal died France was seething with discontent. Richelieu's foreign policy wrecked not only France but most of Europe. His positive achievements cannot be denied. Were they worth all the cost and the suffering caused along the way?

7 Richelieu - For and Against: An Assessment

Historians agree with Richelieu's contemporaries that his death constituted a watershed. Certainly Louis XIII understood its dramatic significance. Although he was heard to laugh heartlessly after visiting the dying man's sick bed, at their last meeting the king was moved by his chief minister's plight, fed him with egg-yolk and refused Richelieu's offer to resign. Louis believed that the great cardinal deserved to die as he had lived, France's chief minister. After the cardinal's death things would never be the same again. As for his life's work, in the words of an English pamphleteer, 'Richelieu was the torment and the ornament of his age'.

So what had Richelieu achieved?

The answer must be, a great deal. According to the same pamphleteer,

'France he subdued, Italy he terrified, Spain he afflicted, Germany he shook'. If Richelieu's priority was the destruction of Habsburg hegemony and Spain's replacement by France as the dominant European power, much spade-work had been done. If there was still a long way to go, the armies of the Habsburgs had been defeated, their rulers humiliated, their economies ruined. Of course this was not all France's doing. Swedes, Dutchmen and Germans had played their part. Gustavus Adolphus' victories were matched by the Dutchman Piet Hein who wrecked the Spanish government's economic plans in 1628 by capturing the annual treasure fleet from the Peruvian silver mines. However, under Richelieu's leadership, France had come to the fore as Spain's chief rival; she had been the lynch-pin of the alliance.

Indeed Richelieu's admirers claim that by the time of his death France was already the great power of the future. Her frontiers had been strengthened by the occupation of Lorraine, the capture of Breisach and the acquisition of Rousillon (see the map on page 123), her armies had been 'blooded', new leaders discovered, and the foundations laid for the organisation which would enable Louis XIV to put half a million men in the field. The French navy had once consisted of an Admiral of France but no ships. Richelieu had abolished the Admiral and conjured up the ships, the dockyards and the sailors. The first steps - hesitant, maybe, but traceable - had been taken towards the foundation of a French empire across the ocean. There is certainly a case for presenting Richelieu as a creative French patriot and nationalist.

Equally profound were the changes accomplished at home. The old interpretation of Richelieu's 'absolutism' oversimplified his policies and exaggerated his achievement. Nevertheless his campaign to build up the authority of the crown had been remarkably successful. First, he had defied and defeated the disruptive forces which had perpetuated political and social instability in France for nearly a century: the embattled Huguenot military establishment, the late-medieval bastard feudalism of the aristocracy, and the presumptuous claims of the *parlements*. Richelieu got his results by building up the king's power-base, both at the centre of government and in the localities. He also established his own position by exploiting the king's favour, by recruiting a totally loyal administrative team, and by intelligent exploitation of patronage. Under the pressures of involvement in the Thirty Years War, from 1635 to 1642, Richelieu created the 'warfare state'. The result was royal authoritarianism or, if you prefer, absolutism. In the service of this state Richelieu dragooned the arts, literature, and the church. He adopted almost a totalitarian attitude; he aimed to capture France's soul. If the term 'great man' means 'someone who radically changed the environment in which he lived', Richelieu was a very great man.

However, all this undoubted achievement does not prevent us asking whether Richelieu's policies were entirely successful and whether they were in the true interests of France and indeed of Europe.

We have seen that to a great extent Richelieu's foreign policy blew up in his face. After the Swedish intervention had led to embarrassment for France and then to a Spanish-imperial victory at Nordlingen, France's direct intervention from 1635 onwards proved to be an expensive fiasco, certainly up until Richelieu's death. Even if invasion and final defeat were averted, there is no way that Richelieu's admirers can argue that everything went according to plan.

Similarly there is a strong case for arguing that Richelieu's domestic policies were hand-to-mouth affairs, creating immense, virtually insoluble problems for his successors. Indeed he timed his death pretty well. We have seen how high the costs were which France had to pay for the experience of being governed by Richelieu. His admirers argue that starvation, fiscal terrorism, bankruptcy, death and bereavement could be justified by ultimate victory over the Habsburgs. To this defence we will turn shortly. However, it can surely be questioned whether France benefited from the establishment of the warfare state, from the manipulation of public opinion, the defiance of the *parlements,* and the establishment of monarchical power. Perhaps this was the only way forward for France. But the case for absolutism should not go through on the nod.

Richelieu also bears much responsibility for the extension and continuation of the Thirty Years War in Europe. All wars are frightful but there is considerable contemporary evidence that this war was exceptionally unpleasant. For example, the artist Jacques Callot depicted otherwise unimaginable horrors: the rows of peasants hanged by looting soldiers while a priest gives absolution to the next man to die, little children resorting to cannibalism, cartloads of nuns being driven off to military brothels. Well might a modern historian, Robert Knecht, liken the spread of the Thirty Years War across the map of Europe to a huge oil slick. It was filthy, obscene, seemingly unstoppable, bringing pollution and death to those it overwhelmed.

To blame Richelieu both for the suffering of the French people, politically bludgeoned and taxed beyond endurance, and for the casualties of the Thirty Years War involves the dangers of moral judgement, hindsight and anachronism. One takes the point that it is unjustifiable to condemn practices which were acceptable in the seventeenth century by late twentieth century standards. To take an obvious example, it might seem shocking and hypocritical to us that a leading exponent of Christianity should enrich himself to the tune of twenty-two million livres, much of this obtained by accumulating church benefices, while France starved. But Richelieu was arguably simply doing what any aristocratic churchman of his day would have done. Similarly, thousands of patriotic Frenchmen no doubt applauded Richelieu's campaign to make France a great power with secure frontiers; only thus could Habsburg encirclement be countered. In the aftermath of Nordlingen and Corbie they would have taken some persuading that 'the decline of Spain' which features in our text-books was really happening. Louis XIII and Richelieu were convinced that Spain was public enemy number one, and to be fair Olivares was just as aggressive and intransigent as Richelieu. Furthermore, it was the aristocrat's calling to respond to such a challenge by fighting. However deplorable war may seem to us or to French or German peasants, that was not how Richelieu's decision-making contemporaries saw it.

And yet! While anachronism must be avoided, there is the opposite danger of assuming that people in the past were stupid, incapable of reasoning and devoid of moral sensitivity. To his credit Louis XIII expressed concern: 'Ah, my poor people, but I cannot relieve them yet of their sufferings because of this war to which I am committed'. Richelieu on the other hand was less compassionate: 'The people must be likened to beasts of burden which are spoilt by too kind treatment'. At Regensburg Tilly's henchman de Flamel remonstrated with Richelieu's diplomat Father Joseph: 'You are a Capuchin, that is to say you are obliged by your profession to do what you can to foster peace in Christendom, and yet you are the man who starts a bloody war - you ought to blush with shame.' Father Joseph demanded an apology and was clearly hurt by such uncomfortably perceptive criticism.

As for Richelieu, the bishop of Lisieux was shocked by the complacent serenity with which the cardinel met his death. One would think that Pope Urban VIII would have had an even more comprehensive overview. He had consistently campaigned for peace between the Catholic powers and had refused a cardinal's hat to Father Joseph because he was a warmonger. His comment on Richelieu's death was as follows: 'Well, if there is a God, Cardinal Richelieu will have much to answer for; if not, he has done very well'. When Louis XIII, on Richelieu's advice, tried to boost France's war effort by placing 'our person, our estate, our crown, and our subjects' under the personal protection of the Virgin Mary, he was reprimanded by the austere and intrepid Saint-Cyran: "There is nothing more capable of offending God than causing religion and piety to serve politics". Clearly, seventeenth century people were fully capable of spotting hypocrisy and of grasping the tragedy of war. They can hardly be accused of anachronism. They were there, they saw what was happening, they experienced the consequences of Richelieu's policies. The French people who lit bonfires when Richeleiu died were similarly guiltless of 'anachronism'.

Another danger seems to be worth avoiding. It must never be assumed that what happened had to happen. Wars occur because of conscious and deliberate decisions taken by rulers and their ministers. As a result of these decisions peace is destroyed by war. 'God send us peace, God in heaven send us peace', pleaded a German peasant in 1629. But European politicians decided otherwise. 'France's rulers had no choice', historians claim. But they did have a choice. Otherwise there would have been no point in Richelieu's memorandum to Louis XIII about Pinerolo (see page 46). 'To be or not to be, that was the question. France chose - existence!' writes an excited French historian, V-L Tapier. Exactly. The truth must surely be that France's rulers had a choice. The question for historians is whether they made the right choice and whether the question really was 'to be or not to be'.

There are undoubtedly questions which should at least be asked. For example, were the rulers of France and Spain really incapable of sorting out their differences without war? Why could the peace of 1627 or of 1630 not have been perpetuated? Was the threat of Habsburg encirclement really so great that only war could prevent it? Was not 'the prevention of Habsburg encirclement' in sober truth code for 'the establishment of French hegemony in Europe'?

We have heard similar stories about 'encirclement' elsewhere. An even more cataclysmic disaster than the Thirty Years War occurred because the Kaiser and his generals purported to believe that their country was 'encircled'. Yet by article 231 of the Versailles Treaty they were branded as war-criminals. It has plausibly been suggested that if every time a war broke out all the diplomats involved were automatically hanged, there would be fewer wars. This glimpse of the obvious certainly applies to World War One, and the historian C.V.Wedgwood has argued that the Thirty Years War was likewise an avoidable and sterile catastrophe: 'Men might have grasped the essential futility of putting the beliefs of the mind to the judgement of the sword'. She goes on to describe the peace of Westphalia as 'a rearrangement of the European map ready for the next war' - ready for the next 'encirclement' dispute, in other words.

Even if we grant that the Habsburg threat to France was not a paper tiger, can this justify the shedding of so much blood? Similarly, it seems strange to argue that the suppression of liberties and the creation of the warfare state in France was the only way forward and that fiscal terrorism was the best method of taxation. Curiously enough, Richelieu's rival, Olivares, introduced radical reforms of taxation in Spain. Even more to the point, in the 1660s Colbert demonstrated that the French 'system' of taxation could be and should be reformed. 'Respect is the death of history', wrote the French historian Michelet. Dare one suggest that Richelieu has received more than his share of respect?

There is a particular reason for scepticism. There is no mystery about where the adulation of Richelieu comes from. It comes from Richelieu. On his deathbed he bade a carefully rehearsed farewell to his king: 'I have the consolation of leaving your kingdom in the highest degree of glory and reputation which it has ever had, and all your enemies beaten and humiliated' - a questionable summary to say the least. Throughout Richelieu's career we have noted his sophisticated exploitation of propaganda on behalf of his country, his monarch and his government's

record and at the expense of his enemies and critics. It is clear that the incense was heaped on Richelieu's altars by Richelieu himself. If the cardinal is nowadays supposed to be 'the greatest servant France ever had', that is exactly what he wrote about himself. Both Richelieu's skill and his self-dedication were stressed in the *Gazette.* On one occasion the proofs arrived of an article describing him as a hero. Richelieu crossed out 'hero' and substituted 'demigod'.

An interesting parallel comes to mind:

> The advanced Soviet science of war received further development at Comrade Stalin's hands. At the various stages of the war Comrade Stalin found the correct solutions. Stalin's military mastery was displayed in defence and offence. Comrade Stalin's genius enabled him to divine the enemy's plans and defeat them. Stalin never allowed his work to be marred by the slightest hint of vanity, conceit or self-adulation.

The author of this report was of course Stalin. Only the last brilliant touch, the claim to modesty, could not be paralleled by Richelieu's writing about himself. Like Stalin the cardinal wrote in order to influence his own contemporaries. He also wrote to influence posterity, for he had a highly developed sense of history. How well he succeeded!

The comparison with Stalin is helpful, for there are other parallels. Since both were trained as priests, they both shared the methodical intellectualism of the seminary. They both had enterprising and far-seeing ideas about the economic futures of their countries. They both played their rivals off against each other and were pitiless in the suppression of opposition. Seguier was Richelieu's Vyshinsky. Stalin's neurotic creation of a mighty power block to ward off the next capitalist attack after the defeat of Hitlerism is reminiscent of Richelieu's obsession with Habsburg encirclement.

Yet even more striking than the parallels between Richelieu and Stalin are contrasts which prompt us to appreciate the case for the cardinal. While Richelieu could be vindictive, he was not paranoid in his suspicions of everyone around him. Nor did he equal Stalin as a mass-murderer, for he was not a monster. Unlike Stalin he had a cultivated and knowledgeable sympathy for the arts. If Richelieu deceived others and perhaps deceived himself about the purity of his motives in serving the state, plenty of other people in history have done the same. Nor was his lust for tyrannical power as crude as Stalin's. And unlike Stalin he ruined his health and worked himself to death in the interests of France, as he understood them. Whether or not readers will entirely accept Richelieu at his own valuation, they may feel that he worked hard for those twenty-two million livres!

To sum up, the comparison between Richelieu and Stalin highlights important aspects of the argument. When we evaluate the achievements of both men, we are in the presence of great power. Both men drastically transformed their environments. Both men did much good - and immense harm. Did the good outweigh the harm or vice versa? No-one would now call Stalin 'the greatest public servant Russia ever had', for the costs of his achievements in terms of human suffering are considered unacceptable. Perhaps it is time to adopt a similarly critical attitude towards Cardinal Richelieu. Maybe Le Grand Armand has got away with it for too long.

Richelieu: Against and For

-	+
European war prolonged	Domination of Europe by France
Suppression of liberties in France	Habsburg powers checked
The Marillac brothers condemned unjustly	French monarchy absolute
Urbain Grandier burnt	Nobles and *parlements* defeated
Devastated and backward economy	Encouragement of the arts
Warfare state - fiscal terrorism	Navy and empire

If there is a God Cardinal Richelieu will have much to answer for
If there is no God he will have done very well

Summary - The Ministry of Cardinal Richelieu, 1624-42

Making notes on *'The Ministry of Cardinal Richelieu'*

This is a favourite topic with examiners. Your essays will reflect the efficiency of your note-making. Concentrate on the various aspects of Richelieu's record - his foreign policy, confrontations with his domestic critics, economic policy, finance, system of government, propaganda. Summarise in chronological form such episodes as the aristocratic plots against Richelieu. Relate these topics to the material in chapters 1 and 2, for instance on patronage and absolutism. Make a businesslike note on Richelieu's achievements and failures, developing the ideas in the flow diagram (see page 82). If you have the necessary interest and expertise, pursue the comparison between Richelieu and Stalin - and also Lenin who is now less reverently regarded even by Russian historians.

Answering essay questions on *'The Ministry of Cardinal Richelieu'*

Consider the following questions:

1 Account for the failure of challenges to royal authority in France between 1624 and 1642.
2 'His first concern was the service of his country'. Discuss this verdict on Richelieu.
3 Evaluate Richelieu's contribution to the construction of an absolutist state in France.
4 In whose interests did Richelieu govern France?
5 'Sensible domestic policies ruined by reckless foreign policies'. Discuss with reference to Richelieu.

To answer these questions you need to have a firm grasp of the chronology and detailed achievements of Richelieu's ministry. The examiner may well accept the orthodox view of Richelieu's merits. Therefore, if you have the chance to be critical, be sure to show yourself fully aware of the case for Richelieu before you consider his faults.

Let us consider question 5. It is a difficult question in that the quotation makes no allowance for the fact that Richelieu's domestic policy was foreign-policy-led. You would have to stress that Richelieu's administrative reforms, economic policies and handling of public opinion were all geared to his ultimate goal, namely the raising of money to finance his wars. Was Richelieu's foreign policy reckless? Don't miss the necessity of dealing with that aspect of the question. Write a clear and explicit conclusion.

Question 3 is certainly worth considering carefully as the issue of Richelieu and absolutism frequently appears on examination papers. In your introduction define absolutism. You could with profit show awareness of the disagreements among historians, but only briefly. In your development prove your familiarity with the nuts and bolts of the 'warfare state'. But stress the limitations of Richelieu's power and success. Don't forget the role of the king in supporting Richelieu. In your conclusion draw your arguments together and clearly answer the question.

Source-based questions on *'The Ministry of Cardinal Richelieu'*

Should Louis XIII or Richelieu accept the responsibility for developments between 1624 and 1643?

Carefully read the documents on pages 46, 57, 67 and 72 (Richelieu's advice to the king about Pinerolo, Louis XIII's expression of his satisfaction, Richelieu's claim to be ignorant about finance, and the exchanges concerning Louis XIII's moods). Answer the following questions:

a) What do you think were Richelieu's own views about Pinerolo? (5 marks)
b) To what extent did Louis XIII maintain a consistent opinion of Richelieu? (5 marks)
c) What do the documents reveal about Louis XIII's personality? (5 marks)
d) What do the sources suggest as to who was the real ruler of France? (10 marks)

You must be very critical of all four documents. Richelieu's claim to know nothing about finance is definitely not to be taken at face value. Louis was always unpredictable and unreliable in his support of Richelieu; he was the king and therefore ultimately the boss. How genuinely did Richelieu think that the king would really choose not to retain Pinerolo? Was Richelieu just flattering the king? With regard to d), do not expect to come up with a clear-cut answer. You will need to conclude that the evidence is contradictory.

CHAPTER 4

The Ministry of Cardinal Mazarin, 1643-61

1 Introduction: the Issues

When Cardinal Richelieu died in December 1642, Louis XIII was mortally ill. His relatively short and painful life ended on 14 May 1643. Rumour had it that the king had been poisoned by Richelieu, but a post mortem found no evidence of foul play. What a tribute to Richelieu that he should be suspected of murdering a victim whom he had predeceased by five months! Louis had accepted Richelieu's advice and had taken the Italian Jules Mazarin into his inner council, though at that stage no-one was specifically named as chief minister. Aware that his own time was running out, Louis was preoccupied with what would happen after his death when France would be ruled by his four year old son. The dying king's chief worry was that the wife whom he had despised and humiliated for nearly thirty years would become regent. So he made a will and had it registered by the Paris *parlement* by which Anne would be but one of a regency council. Louis' intention was that she would be controlled by its other members - her brother-in-law Gaston d'Orléans, Condé the senior prince of the blood, and four ministers - and that decisions would be taken by a majority vote.

However, not even Louis the Just could rule from his urn. Only four days after his death that same *parlement*, informed that it was the little king's wish that his mother should rule, overturned the will and made Anne sole regent. She soon made it clear that she would not be a cipher and had worked out how to play the difficult role of queen-regent. She had selected Mazarin as her collaborator. Together they now moved in on her late-husband's nominees. Before Louis' death Mazarin and Chavigny had procured the dismissal of Sublet de Noyers - on the grounds that he was conspiring to make Anne regent! Now Chavigny was disgraced as well. Anne of Austria disliked Chavigny because he brought back memories of the wretched time she had had during Richelieu's ministry. Gaston was fobbed off with the resounding title of Lieutenant General of the Kingdom while Condé was dispatched to the front to win more victories. That left Mazarin whom Anne liked very much. So she made him chief minister, a post he was to occupy with brief intermissions until his death eighteen years later.

Thus Mazarin exercised responsiblity for France's destiny for the same number of years as Richelieu. On the whole the French people agreed with Cardinal de Retz - whom we shall meet again. Richelieu he disliked but respected, Mazarin he neither liked nor respected. Throughout his career, according to de Retz, Mazarin 'kept Machiavelli by his bedside as well as his breviary'; he had tricked his way to the top and by trickery he stayed there. Historians have treated Mazarin more generously. Their consensus is that he was an adequate successor to Richelieu if not quite in the same class.

In the following sections we shall discuss this verdict. We shall evaluate the challenges facing Mazarin. To what extent did he have choices when selecting his policies? Were the policies he chose in the interests of the French people? In particular, Mazarin is associated with the great crisis known as the Fronde which afflicted France between 1648 and 1653. Did Mazarin make unforced errors which brought this crisis upon the French people, or was it the more or less inevitable result of Richelieu's costly imperialism? Did the Frondeurs offer a viable alternative to the political system built up by Richelieu and Mazarin? How well did France, guided by Mazarin, recover from the traumas of the Fronde?

As with Richelieu, Mazarin's own strengths and weaknesses, his priorities and perceptions, his background and his personality markedly affected events during his tenure of power. It is therefore to his personality that we now turn. What sort of a man was Mazarin?

2 Mazarin: the Man

Guilio Mazzarini, or Jules Mazarin as he was known in France, was born 14 July 1602 and brought up in Rome. His parents belonged to the minor aristocracy. Young Jules benefited from the patronage of the great Colonna family, before achieving success as a diplomat in the papal service. But his career really took off when he impressed Richelieu with his courage and intelligence. As we have seen, Mazarin displayed these qualities when he managed to halt the fighting between the French and the Spanish at Casale in 1630 (see page 46). Richelieu let it be known that young Mazarin would be welcome at the French court as the papal nuncio - an office he performed with finesse from 1634 to 1636. Back at Rome, he defended French interests as a secret agent until in 1639 he was recalled to France to join Richelieu's circle of familiars. Although he never proceeded beyond deacon's orders, he was made a cardinal in 1641 thanks to French pressure. Mazarin earned his promotion by defusing a dangerous situation in Savoy provoked by Louis XIII's sister Christine who was imprudently and flamboyantly unfaithful to her husband, Duke Amadaus. He was closely involved in the unmasking of the Cinq Mars conspiracy, and personally received the fortress of Sedan from the disgraced Bouillon (see page 60). He may well have saved both the queeen and Gaston d'Orleans from disgrace as well. Such a useful operator was marked for further promotion.

How had Mazarin achieved such success in a country which was virulently xenophobic? Partly because of his remarkable ability. He was a very clever man, every bit as devious as Richelieu and capable of the utmost dissimulation. 'Will they acclaim me?', Christine asked Mazarin when he escorted her back to Savoy. 'I have no idea, Madame, but we must appear to relish whatever words they fling at us'. Mazarin was also well aware that the capacity to be underestimated is one of the politician's most valuable skills. So he smiled to himself when his rivals despised him for his apparent humility and diffidence. But they were mistaken, for Mazarin was not a diffident man at all. He was intensely ambitious, enjoying both the acquisition and exercise of power and also the good things which power brings in its train. The passage of time would show what a brilliant accumulator of wealth and influence France was nursing in her bosom.

Another part of the explanation for Mazarin's success is that he was very amiable. He made himself agreable as well as useful to people who mattered. For example, Richelieu, who was not easily charmed, was obviously very fond of his *'Nunziniardo'* ('dear little nuncio'). Mazarin

Cardinal Mazarin, by an unknown artist

made him laugh - again, no easy feat. 'Signor Jules' was a welcome visitor to the contrasting establishments of the ascetic Father Joseph and the hedonistic Chavigny. It was typical of Mazarin that he made a habit of sending presents to his influential French friends; for instance when he was in Rome, he bought jewels for Anne of Austria and pictures for Richelieu.

'What a creep!', you may think - but such a judgement would not be wholly fair. While there was no doubt an element of calculation in Mazarin's cultivation of the great and the good, he was a genuinely sociable and friendly man of the world. He liked to be liked. Furthermore, there really was a nice side to him. 'I am not malicious by nature' he justly claimed. It is to his credit that by no means all the people whom he benefited were rich and aristocratic. For instance, once he had 'arrived' at the French court he vigorously promoted the interests of his poor friends and relations back in Rome.

Nor should we doubt that Mazarin's cordial relationship with the queen originated in genuine kindness and sympathy. 'To a gentleman any country is his homeland', Mazarin once wrote. But he and the queen knew from first-hand experience that Frenchmen were not always so internationally minded. Both were attracted to each other as foreigners in a strange and at times inhospitable land. Contemporaries and historians have even suggested that Mazarin and Anne were secretly married. As Mazarin was only in minor orders, this would not have been impossible. They were certainly fond of each other. 'Yours to the last breath', was how he used to end his letters to her.

Mazarin, it must be admitted, was something of a scalliwag. He paid for his friends' presents with his winnings at the gaming table where he was notoriously lucky. He always won and probably cheated; it is appropriate that his family papers are lodged at Monte Carlo. But Mazarin was much more than a mere adventurer. It is now time to discover whether this urbane and plausible man of the world, so adept at looking after himself, could look after a great nation. Was he a statesman or just a clever politician?

3 Mazarin's Foreign Policy

a) Objectives

Mazarin was too fond of the good life to be a war-monger and it was not insignificant that his first irruption onto the stage of history had been in a peace-making role (see page 46). Furthermore the queen was anxious that peace should be restored between her adoptive country and the land of her birth. Meanwhile domestic reform and the mitigation of the taxes necessitated by war depended on a speedy termination of hostilities, for in a cruelly real sense, Mazarin's domestic policies were - like Richelieu's - foreign-policy-led. Obviously it was in everyone's interest to scale down 'fiscal terrorism' and 'the warfare state', the unacceptable features of Richelieu's absolutism. But that could only happen when victory had been won or at least a satisfactory settlement achieved. So there is every reason to believe that Mazarin was sincere in his attempts to bring Richelieu's horrendous wars to a prompt and favourable conclusion. This was undoubtedly his supreme objective.

But such a goal proved elusive. Perhaps there is no better illustration of the adage that it is easier to start than to end a war than Mazarin's frustrated and despairing attempts to achieve a victorious peace between 1643 and 1659. It is indeed sadly ironic that Mazarin should have been attacked by his French critics for deliberately prolonging the wars which he had inherited. There was little truth in this accusation, though it was believed at the time. But the terms for any settlement with the Habsburg powers had to be right. Mazarin's credibility with the French political nation, to say nothing of the queen's, would have been demolished by a sell-out. It was known that Mazarin and Anne of Austria corresponded in Spanish, and a suspicious and uncharitable public opinion would never have forgiven an apparent sacrifice of French interests to Spain and the Empire. So Mazarin's immediate goal was military. Only success on the battle-field would persuade the Habsburgs to enter into serious negotiations through which Mazarin's diplomatic skills could achieve the desired results. In the meantime the bayonet and the bullet ruled.

b) The Peace of Westphalia - a Flawed Achievement

We saw in the last chapter that France's intervention in the Thirty Years War did not transform her into a formidable military power. Far from it. Inefficiency, corruption, and insubordination typified the French army. This continued to be so during Mazarin's ministry. Very slowly and haltingly, able administrators such as Le Tellier brought order out of chaos, while Condé and Turenne provided better leadership. But it took time. Therefore, while Condé's victories at Rocroi (19 May 1643), Freiburg (30 June 1644) and Lens (20 August 1648) are rightly famous, for the most part the war was inconclusive. Disorderly mobs posing as armies blundered around Germany and France's northern frontiers, sometimes besieging towns that were unlucky enough to be in the way, but more often ravaging the countryside and subjecting the peasantry to rape, murder and pillage.

Gradually, however, the fact that France was slightly less exhausted than everyone else paid off. France's control of the Rhine was tightened by Condé's recapture of Philippsburg and Turenne's storming of Worms and Mainz. And Turenne linked with the Swedish army under Wrangel in order to invade Bavaria in 1646. In May 1648 they decisively defeated the Imperialist-Bavarian army at Süsmarshausen and invaded Austria. Vienna and Prague were now threatened. Meanwhile, French troops fought alongside Portuguese and Catalonian rebels against the King of Spain who was now hard put to defend his own Iberian peninsula from political disintegration.

It might be thought that these victories by France and her allies would bring the Habsburgs to the negotiating table. Actually they had been there for some time. The decision to hold a peace conference had been taken as long ago as 1641, though the delegates of the European powers did not begin to arrive at Münster and Osnabrück, the designated conference towns, until 1643. Then for five years diplomats haggled about procedure and protocol while people throughout Europe starved and bled. It is an excellent example of war being prolonged by men who were not in the firing-line.

Why should they hurry? The Danish ambassador sent for his wife, the Venetian ambassador planted a garden. The diplomats required two separate venues because the Swedes and the French would not give precedence to each other, so the Imperialists negotiated with the French at Münster and with the Swedes at Osnabrück. The French ambassador, the duc de Longueville, would not make the initial approach to the Spanish ambassador, the duke of Peneranda, and *vice versa* since to do so would implicitly concede precedence. France would not recognise the King of Spain's title as King of Portugal, nor would Spain acknowledge the King of France as King of Navarre. The papal representatives would not sit down with heretics, while the Spanish were reluctant to talk to Dutch rebels. The emperor refused to tolerate Protestantism in his hereditary lands, while the Swedes wanted an electorate for themselves - in order to safeguard Protestanism. All these and countless other disputes were conducted in Latin by hundreds of lawyers. It is astonishing that anything was achieved.

The diplomats were eventually jolted out of their complacent gyrations by an amazing event. In January 1648 the Spanish and the Dutch went behind everyone's backs and signed a peace treaty all on their own. The United Provinces now finally achieved their independence from Spain while the Spanish achieved a notable coup by detaching the Dutch from the French camp. This dramatic development, highly unwelcome to the French, was in fact Mazarin's fault. He himself had tried to negotiate with the Spaniards behind his Dutch ally's back - and the Spaniards had revealed all to the Dutch. Mazarin's representative Servien who had replaced the haughty Longueville conspired with the Elector of Bavaria to punish the Spaniards by excluding them from further negotations while a settlement was achieved with the Empire. The outbreak of the Fronde (see next section) prompted the regent and her chief minister to recommend haste at Münster. The treaty between France and the Emperor was signed on 24 October 1648, the treaty between the Protestant states and the Emperor at Osnabrück a week later. The Thirty Years War had at last ended.

What sort of a settlement did Mazarin achieve for France? Her possession of Metz, Toul, Verdun, Breisach and Pinerolo was confirmed (see the map on page 123). She was given the right to garrison Philippsburg. However, the terms relating to Alsace were unsatisfactorily vague. The great city and fortress of Strasbourg remained within the Empire, although France obtained 'full sovereignty' over Upper and Lower Alsace, including ten important towns (Colmar, Hagenau, Schlettstadt, Weissenburg, Landau, Oberenheim, Rosheim, Münster, Kaiserburg and Turinckheim). But the nobility of Alsace and the ten towns retained their privileges vis-à-vis the Empire 'provided that' these privileges did not diminish French sovereignty. The Latin words for 'provided that' *(ita tamen)* were to cause endless arguments in the future. Was Alsace French or not? It was even suggested that Mazarin deliberately chose such sloppy phrasing so that it could be exploited in future diplomatic confrontations.

Valuable though these territorial acquisitions unquestionably were, the concessions made by the Emperor to Sweden, Brandenburg and the German princes represented an even greater triumph for France. How Richelieu's ghost must have chuckled! France successfully demanded that the Electors, Princes and imperial cities should be represented at the conference. There they finally achieved their independence from imperial control. So much for Habsburg imperialism. Equally galling for Ferdinand III was the concession of toleration not only to Lutheran but also to Calvinist rulers. Why should this please Catholic France? Because the dreams of Habsburg imperialists had always had a religious dimension. Not only had these been defeated, but it was entirely apparent whom the Germans and Swedes had to thank for their political and religious liberty. France was clearly established as the protector of 'German liberties', that is to say the diffuse hotch-potch of crazy principalities and powers that was to be a substitute for a German state until Bismarck overturned the Westphalia settlement in 1870-71.

In other words, France now dominated Western Europe. Whether this undoubted achievement was worth all the cost in human and material terms that had been inflicted by the war is another matter. Mazarin's French critics were not impressed. They believed that the wily Italian had only come to terms with France's enemies because his government was under such pressure at home. And anyway, why was there still no settlement with Spain? While we may acquit Mazarin of the charge of dragging his feet over negotiations with the Empire, we can nevertheless agree that the failure to settle with Spain was regrettable. It meant that for France the peace of Westphalia did not bring peace. Another decade of futile and costly war proved to be necessary before hostilities ended with the Spanish Habsburgs.

c) The Road to the Pyrenees, 1648-59

Historians used to represent the 1650s as a serene and constructive time.

Inside France the Fronde had been defeated and the enemies of the crown had been put to flight. Externally the shrewd Italian cardinal engineered a triumphant end to the centuries-old conflict with Spain. French victories led logically to the Treaty of the Pyrenees in 1659, and to Louis XIV's marriage with Philip IV's daughter, Maria Theresa. All was now set for the reign of the Sun King.

We now know that it was not like that. The 1650s were in fact wretched years in which France seethed with discontent. Suffering at home and frustration abroad were the hallmarks of this period. We shall shortly proceed to the Fronde and discover that the problems which caused this traumatic movement of protest were by no means speedily resolved. This truth is highly relevant to our study of Mazarin's foreign policy. For France's internal difficulties - first, the Fronde, then continuing gestures of defiance - encouraged the Spanish government to continue the war. Spain had serious problems too. But as long as France stumbled, it was a game of 'chicken': who would give way first?

Significantly, in her search for support, France had to swallow her pride and recognise the English republic. This did not come naturally. French public opinion unanimously condemned the execution in 1649 of Charles I who had after all been married to Louis XIII's sister. In addition, the French economy was damaged by an English trade embargo in 1649. There was also worrying evidence that Cromwell was willing to support the Frondeurs of Bordeaux. Yet relations with London were never completely severed and the trade war was concluded. This provoked the publication in Paris of a scurrilous pamphlet which, according to an English observer, showed Cromwell sitting on his commode 'at his business and the King of Spain on the one side and the King of France on the other, offering him paper to wipe his breech'.

France's desperate need for allies was illustrated by the Spanish capture of Dunkirk on 16 September 1652. The French commander, the Comte d'Estrades, had made it clear to his government that he would surrender if his garrison did not receive supplies. Mazarin therefore organised a French fleet of eight warships and sixteen transports which it was hoped would solve d'Estrades' problems. However, the relieving fleet was set upon by a joint Anglo-Spanish force, commanded by Admiral Blake. Seven out of the eight French warships were sunk or captured and all the French transports were captured or turned round and dispersed. No French army was within fifty miles of Dunkirk and so d'Estrades surrendered. This disaster was a humiliation for France's army, navy and diplomacy. Clearly on her own she was a spent force.

But allies were hard to find. The last thing the Dutch wanted was war against Spain. Germany was exhausted. The Scandinavian powers were too remote to tackle the Spaniards. So it was eventually republican England that helped France break out of isolation. The Treaty of Westminster signed on 3 November 1655 was officially a trade agreement. But in a secret clause Cromwell promised not to give asylum to exiled Frondeurs while Mazarin undertook to expel James, Duke of York (Charles II had already departed for Cologne). This treaty led two years later to a full-blown military alliance against Spain.

Thus the Most Catholic King recruited Protestant English republicans in order to defeat the French queen's brother, King Philip IV. At the battle of the Dunes (14 June 1658) 6,500 vigorous, well-fed, well-equipped English redcoats helped Turenne to rout the Spanish while an efficient English fleet blockaded Dunkirk. The Spaniards were forced to surrender Gravelines to France, and soon afterwards Louis XIV made a triumphal entry into Dunkirk which was then promptly handed over to England. Although Louis XIV would buy back Dunkirk from England in 1662, this campaign hardly redounded to France's credit. Her much-vaunted armies - vaunted that is by historians - were seemingly incapable of delivering a knock-out blow on their own.

Nor was Mazarin successful in bringing pressure to bear on Spain elsewhere. The Habsburg cause was strengthened by the imperial election of 1658 when Leopold I succeeded his father, Ferdinand III. Mazarin had advanced the claims of Louis XIV to be the seventeenth-century version of the Emperor Charlemagne, but to no avail. In order to counteract this disappointment Mazarin encouraged the electors to form the League of the Rhine in defence of German liberties, and indeed France became a member. This was an intelligent development of Richelieu's policy of supporting and encouraging the German princes to defy their emperor. But it was doubtful if Madrid was impressed by the meetings of the League's Council at Frankfurt which were to die of apathy in 1668. Nor did Mazarin's plans to challenge Spanish control of Italy yield results. His attempt to encourage a revolt in Naples failed - in Mazarin's words, *'un frutto non maturo'*.

However, Mazarin had one supreme trump card. Louis XIV was Europe's most eligible bachelor. Whom would he marry? This question fascinated both friend and foe. Louis' father had married the king of Spain's daughter. And now another king of Spain offered another daughter. What a splendid way to end a war in which both contestants were on their knees, but too proud to admit it. Of course the terms would have to be right and some hard bargaining would be necessary. Ever since marriage between Louis and Maria Theresa had been first mooted in 1654, the Spaniards had played hard to get. They were finally brought to the negotiating table by a splendid piece of theatre. Mazarin ostentatiously broadcast the possibility of Louis' betrothal to Marguerite, the daughter of the Duke of Savoy. In October 1658 the court travelled south to Lyons so that Louis could meet Marguerite and terms could be finalised. The Spaniards were horrified and immediately dispatched representatives to Lyons with full powers to negotiate. Mazarin's ruse had worked, for the marriage with Maria Theresa was promptly agreed in principle and only the details remained to be settled.

Marguerite was heart-broken, but she was dispensable, for compared with Spain Savoy was a tinpot power. In the meantime Mazarin's diplomat Lionne on behalf of the Most Christian King and Don Louis de Haro on behalf of the Most Catholic King got down to business on the Isle of Pheasants providentially sited in the middle of the river Bidaossa which separates France from Spain.

The orthodox view is that the Treaty of the Pyrenees was Mazarin's crowning glory, the final consummation of the programme so doggedly pursued by both the great cardinals. Certainly Richelieu would have approved of the confirmation of France's conquests: Rousillon and Cerdagne in the south, Artois, Gravelines, Landrecies, Avesnes, Thionville in the north and Montmédy in Luxemburg (see the map on page 123). Furthermore the marriage of Louis and Maria Theresa offered dazzling propects for the future. While Maria Theresa renounced her claim to the Spanish succession, this was dependent on the payment of a dowry of 500,000 crowns. Given the parlous state of the Spanish treasury, it was probable that the dowry would never be paid. So Maria Theresa's claims to the Spanish empire would stand - and so would her children's. It was already on the cards that 'the Pyrenees had ceased to exist' as the Spanish ambassador remarked forty years later when Louis' and Maria Theresa's grandson became King Philip V of Spain.

In several respects, however, the Pyrenees settlement was a compromise. In return for Spain's renunciation of Alsace, France abandoned her claim to Catalonia and left her Portuguese allies to survive as best they could. Condé, the traitor, was pardoned and his lands restored to him. Lorraine was to be restored to its duke, although his army was demobilised. There was no question of Spain publicly admitting defeat or implicitly conceding European hegemony to France.

Now all was set for the most brilliant marriage of the century. The French court made stately progress south towards the Pyrenees. At Aix-en-Provence Louis heard that his uncle Gaston had died, leaving him his books and medals, while at the same time Condé knelt in homage and penitence. Louis forgave him and invited him to the wedding - an invitation which Condé politely declined. So the death of one trouble-maker coincided with the surrender of another. The bridal couple eventually met on the Isle of Pheasants and in the presence of Philip IV and Anne of Austria were married on 9 June 1660. After Marie Theresa had taken tearful leave of her father, the French court headed north for a ceremonial entry into Paris. Mazarin's work was done. He considered entering the priesthood so that he could become pope. But death intervened before the master of diplomacy could fix that little matter as well. There was to be no Pope Jules.

How successful was Mazarin's foreign policy? If we accept that his aims were to bring the war against the Habsburg powers to a satisfactory conclusion, then clearly he was successful. The threat of Habsburg encirclement had been finally scotched. The Emperor's power in Germany was limited by the concessions extracted at Westphalia and by the League of the Rhine. French had now replaced Spanish hegemony in Europe. France's frontiers had become much more secure due to the acquisition of Rousillon in the south, Alsace in the east and strategic fortresses in the north. Lorraine was neutralised, the Dutch, the Swedish and the English were friendly. The Peace of the Pyrenees offered exciting prospects of future French aggrandizement.

But it had taken so long to get there! That is the crux of the case against Mazarin's foreign policy. If the treaties of Westphalia and the Pyrenees were indeed creditable achievements, they had cost France years of bloodshed, suffering and financial exhaustion. Could this have been avoided? Could Mazarin have achieved his results more quickly? We shall never know, though there is no harm in asking the question. Arguably, given Habsburg obstinacy and Spain's resources, ultimate victory was by no means inevitable and was bound to take time and be extremely costly. Were there available alternatives for Mazarin to pursue? Probably not. Mazarin had less choice than Richelieu, for he was not a free agent. He inherited policies, obligations and problems from his predecessor. The most intractable of these problems was France's inability to fund a sufficiently formidable military campaign to bring Spain to her knees. It was a hard problem to solve.

In the event Mazarin's diplomacy compensated for France's military weakness. By calling in Protestant England just as Richelieu had called in Protestant Sweden, Mazarin ended the war and achieved a settlement. And, to be fair, what a settlement! Strategically Mazarin set things up very nicely for Louis XIV: a power vacuum in western Europe which an ambitious and unscrupulous ruler of an eventually revitilised France could brilliantly exploit. But the emasculation of France's potential rivals was only achieved at immense cost to the French people. To that story we now turn.

4 Mazarin's Domestic Policy - the Fronde

a) The Background to the Fronde (1643-8)

Between 1648 and 1653 France was disrupted by the revolts and disturbances known as the Fronde. Fronde means a sling or catapult. Such a weapon was used by Paris urchins to hurl stones at the windows of the rich. As the Fronde began in Paris, the revolts acquired this collective name. However, historians who argue that the Fronde was so called because it was trivial are too ingenious. For the Fronde was not trivial. It was the most dangerous challenge to royal authority between the sixteenth-century Wars of Religion and the French Revolution of 1789. The American historian F. Lloyd Moote argues that 'both geographically and socially the Fronde was the most widespread of all the rebellions in mid-seventeenth-century Europe'.

Why did the Fronde occur? It was caused by problems, many of them bequeathed by Richelieu, and by mistakes committed by Mazarin.

An immediate problem was the resentment provoked by Mazarin as chief minister. It was not simply that he was an Italian who was ruling Frenchmen. Even more objectionable was the system, initiated by Richelieu, whereby the chief minister monopolised power and patronage to the exclusion of the aristocracy. In 1643-4 indignant and self-regarding aristocrats, denied both power at the centre of the state and provincial governerships, plotted Mazarin's assassination. Their attempted coup, known as *l'affaire des importants,* was led by the duc de Beaufort. This volatile nobleman was the son of Vendôme, one of Henri IV's bastards. Popular with the Paris mob, he had acquired the nickname *le roi des halles,* (the king of the markets). Beaufort's revolt failed because government spies found out about it. Judicious arrests proved that Mazarin could protect his own back. Nevertheless the *importants* served notice that high-born Frenchmen would not accept their exclusion from office. Beaufort escaped from prison four years later to play a leading part in the Fronde.

Even more worrying was the financial situation. It was noted in the last chapter that Richelieu and his colleagues proved incapable of funding satisfactorily the expensive war against the Habsburg powers. In 1642 the war cost the treasury 88 million livres. This went up to 120 million in 1643 and 136 million in 1645. The government's debts exceeded 100 million livres. Mazarin's solution was to gamble. He borrowed recklessly in the hope that he would win the war quickly. Victory would settle the debt - a huge war indemnity to be paid by the vanquished, newly conquered provinces to plunder, and Spanish gold flowing into Parisian vaults. Like Richelieu, Mazarin pretended to be ignorant about finance while subordinates administered the details and took the blame. Mazarin's frontman was the corrupt, unimpressive Superintendent of Finances, Particelli d'Emeri. Undoubtedly with Mazarin's approval, d'Emeri borrowed on a massive scale at interest rates of between 15 and 20 percent. For instance, he borrowed 115 million livres in 1645, anticipating the crown's revenues until the end of 1647. This was financial madness unless victory intervened.

Alas, for once Cardinal Mazarin's celebrated luck ran out. While the Emperor and the King of Spain had their own financial problems, they knew all about Mazarin's. As we have seen, the French armies were incapable of inflicting decisive defeats on their opponents. So a slogging-match ensued which the Imperialists and the Spaniards financed in their own equally hand-to-mouth way. He who endured to the end would be saved. But it was not clear that it would be France.

The trouble was that it was not just a question of money. In order to raise revenue the government was rapidly using up its reserves of goodwill. Initially there was relief when Richelieu's death was soon followed by that of the sombre tyrant, Louis the Just. There had been sympathy for the queen regent and for her apparent willingness to appeal to the *Parlement*. Before long, however, the continuation of the war, the ever-increasing taxes, the regent's own high-handedness, and above all the monopoly of power by the slimy Italian made the government disliked by all. For instance, on Mazarin's advice four judges who opposed the levying of the toisé (a tax on buildings outside the walls of Paris) were imprisoned in March 1645. Their leader, President Barillon, died in prison and became a martyr for the opposition. Anne would not listen to advice from conservatives such as Matthew Molé, First President of the *Parlement* of Paris:

> One can say to Your Majesty that the greatest advantage a sovereign can possess consists in reigning always by love over his subjects, that he cannot commit a graver mistake than to have himself continually obeyed through terror; it is a fatal moment when the majesty which is graven on his countenance, which alone separates him from common men, is not respected for the tender and true sentiments which it conveys to the hearts of the people.

Anne was foolish to resent and ignore such well-meant advice, for its salient feature was its royalism. Instead she listened to Mazarin.

Anne of Austria and Mazarin lacked Richelieu's ability to manipulate public opinion. They failed to explain why the war could not be ended, why it cost so much, why new sources of revenue had to be exploited. So French people believed the worst. They were naturally xenophobic in any case. A foreigner in charge of their government was bad enough, high taxation exacted and exploited by the odious financiers (whose popular nickname was 'the snakes') was worse, but a foreigner who was allegedly making a fortune out of his friendships with those same financiers was intolerable. No wonder he was prolonging the war!

Perhaps Mazarin's most provocative blunder was to alienate the office-holders. Although Richelieu had caused offence by his reliance on *intendants* who appropriated office-holders' powers and profits, he never forgot the government's natural supporters. By propaganda and patronage he retained the loyalty of the office-holders, playing them off against the financiers. Now the picture changed. Protests by senior office-holders such as the trésuriers de France showed how Mazarin had lost their support by 1648:

> The *intendants* of the provinces and the financiers of the *taille* have reduced the *trésoriers de France* of all the *generalités* of the Kingdom to a miserable state by removing them from their functions (which the *intendants* have usurped absolutely) and by the violent seizure of their salaries by the tax collectors. These *intendants* and

> financiers have united not only for the ruination of the *trésoriers de France,* but all the other office-holders in the provinces, and have so unreasonably conducted themselves that they seem to have undertaken the general destruction of the provinces of the Kingdom to which they have been sent, and have committed so many misappropriations, peculations, fleecings and other violent actions that as a result of the great number of these abuses the state has fallen into the necessity in which it now finds itself.

By January 1648 the unfortunate d'Emeri was at his wits' end. The government's credit was so low that even the financiers would only lend at exorbitant rates. Whatever d'Emeri tried rebounded. Mazarin even agreed that the rich should be taxed. The hated *toisé* clearly damaged the wretches who lived in the slums outside the walls, but it hit their landlords too who were invariably the Parisian bourgeois. Barillon suffered and died for both rich and poor. New tariffs on goods entering Paris provoked riots. When the government announced that the *rentes* paid to investors in government bonds would be halved, the rentiers formed a committee to guard their interests. Finding the money was becoming harder every day.

On 15 January 1648 the government took the desperate step of enforcing six new fiscal edicts by means of a *lit de justice,* held in the presence of the king and the queen mother at the Palais Royal. This approach was necessary as the judges in the *Parlement* would never have willingly accepted d'Emeri's proposals - the creation of twelve new *maîtres des requêtes,* not because they were needed but purely to raise revenue, the imposition of the *franc-fief* (a complicated fine on feudal property acquired by non-nobles), plus new purchase taxes on food and wine sold in Paris. These taxes were exceptionally unwelcome as Paris was starving and the winter was the worst in living memory, the Seine having frozen. The little king who was recovering from smallpox and had to be carried into the Great Chamber had learnt his speech by heart. But he forgot his lines and wept with mortification. As for the queen mother, 'the only man in the government' as some wit remarked, tears welled up in her eyes too at an insolent speech by Omar Talon, the Advocate General. He recommended registration of the edicts but blamed the government for France's sufferings. The atmosphere was sullen as the judges reluctantly complied, and there were no shouts of '*Vive le roi!*' when the royal party left. During the next few weeks the judges amended the government's edicts, considerably reducing the money to be raised by the *franc-fief.*

Mazarin now committed a disastrous blunder. He tried to split the opposition by exploiting the *Paulette* (see page 9). The renewal of this tax which occurred every nine years was due shortly. The government announced that to retain their rights to pass on their offices members of three sovereign courts in Paris (the *Cour des Aides,* the *Chambre des*

Comptes and the *Grand Conseil)* and of provincial *parlements* should surrender their salaries for four years instead of paying the usual one sixtieth of the value of their office, but this burden would *not* be imposed on the *Parlement* of Paris. This crude attempt to play the courts off against each other rebounded. On 13 May 1648 all the sovereign courts decided by an *arrêt de union* (edict of union) to send delegates to a joint assembly in the Chambre Saint Louis of the Palais de Justice. This assembly proposed a number of radical reforms: the suppression of the *intendants,* the reduction of the *taille* by a third, a *chambe de justice* to investigate the conduct of the financiers, the *parlements* henceforth to be consulted about taxation, *lettres de cachet* to be abolished and arrested persons to be tried within twenty-four hours.

While Anne of Austria was livid ('this is sheer republicanism!'), Mazarin, more intelligent and realistic, appreciated that concessions were unavoidable. On 9 July the Superintendent of Finances, the unpopular d'Emeri, was replaced by Marshal de La Meilleraie, an honest soldier. On 31 July at a *lit de justice* the proposals of the Chambre Saint Louis were accepted by the government. The *intendants* were abolished except in the frontier provinces and the *taille* was reduced.

Then news arrived from the front: Condé had defeated the Spaniards at Lens. Mazarin allowed this triumph to unbalance his judgement. Now, he concluded, was the psychologically correct time for an offensive. Strong-arm tactics would prevail. Condé's victory justified a *Te Deum* (thanksgiving to God) at Notre Dame on the morning of 26 August. For this ceremony troops were automatically paraded as a body-guard for the royal family. Why not use these troops to arrest prominent trouble-makers? Mazarin's decision to appeal to force turned a political confrontation into a civil war. The Fronde had begun.

What caused the Fronde? Certainly Richelieu bequeathed virtually insoluble problems: an unfinished war, the treasury in debt, a population seething with discontent. However, there are limits to which people can be blamed for disasters after their deaths; Bismarck was not wholly to blame for Hitler. Mazarin had turned a crisis into a rebellion by uniting against the government the senior magistrates of the robe and the ordinary office-holders. The point needs re-emphasising: these people were normally the crown's most consistent supporters. One cannot imagine Richelieu making such an elementary blunder. Now Mazarin compounded his mistakes by turning the leaders of this dangerous coalition into heroes and martyrs. As a result, he had the people of Paris to deal with as well. This situation was exploited by Mazarin's aristocratic enemies. He was in trouble.

b) The *Fronde Parlementaire* (August 1648 - March 1649)

Anyone who claims fully to understand the Fronde has probably got it wrong. For in truth it was an exceptionally complex episode about which many questions remain unanswered. For one thing, while there was a continuous sequence of crises and disturbances between 1648 and 1653, trouble flared up all over France, now here, now there, and with varying intensity and with apparent lack of logic. Contemporaries were bewildered, while historians of the Fronde disagree in their explanations, assessments and interpretations.

It has been customary to distinguish between the *Fronde Parlementaire* (August 1648 - March 1649) and the *Fronde des Princes* (January 1650 - February 1653). This is clearly an oversimplification, as the magistrates continued to play a part long after March 1649, while the aristocracy were involved in the revolt of autumn 1648. However, there is some validity in the distinction which, on balance, is probably more help than hindrance. (See the summary of events on page 118).

Mazarin's confrontation with the *Parlement* of Paris brought matters to a head. While there was certainly an element of selfishness in the magistrates' opposition, the *Parlement* of Paris was widely accepted as the authentic expression of the nation's grievances. So, when Anne of Austria and Mazarin decided to go onto the offensive and victimise prominent *parlementaires,* they found that they had a revolt on their hands. There was outrage in Paris when the king's guards arrested Pierre Broussel, one of the most respected and outspoken of the government's critics in the *Parlement,* who lived in relative poverty due to his generosity to the poor. Shocked bystanders watched as the old man - he was seventy-two - was dragged from his lunch-table and, still wearing his carpet-slippers, bundled into a carriage and driven off to prison. President Blancmesnel was also arrested, while President Charton who had pleaded for tax reductions escaped the guards by jumping over his garden wall. But it was Broussel's name that spread like wild-fire through the city - 'Broussel is taken!'. The tocsin was rung (an alarm conveyed by ringing church bells). Barricades of paving-stones, barrels, carts and beams sprang up in the narrow streets. The bourgeois militia mobilised. Shop-keepers put up their shutters. A mob of artisans surged towards the Notre Dame bridge, shouting 'Long live the king, and liberty for Broussel'. When Marshal de La Meilleraie, in command of the king's guards, attempted to restore order, his men were pelted from the roof tops. Despite his decision to fire on the crowds, he had to withdraw ignominiously.

Now there emerged one of the Fronde's 'characters', Paul de Gondi. He was Coadjutor (assistant) to his uncle, the Archbishop of Paris, and was later raised to the purple as Cardinal de Retz. Gondi had a journalist's flair for publicity and a kind heart - he sent firewood to the exiled queen of England, Henrietta Maria, during the winter of 1648-9 because she was too poor to afford a fire. He once described himself as 'the least ecclesiastical person in the world', though when beaten by a rival to a lady's affections he remarked, 'just the sort of thing that *would* happen to a saint'. It never ceased to amaze him that he was not chief minister, for Gondi was totally lacking in self-awareness. This unconventional cleric was tidying up after the *Te Deum* when he heard about the barricades. Immediately he sallied forth to 'quell the riot'. However, Gondi found this beyond him, and he was jostled and jeered. But after he had given absolution in the street to one of de La Meilleraie's dying victims, the rioters adopted him as their spokesman. Eventually the Coadjutor, still in his robes, led the crowd to the Palais Royal 'to tell the queen to release Broussel'.

Here the Coadjutor's ego-trip ended. Anne of Austria detested Gondi as a libertine and a trouble-maker. She rejected his plea for the release of Broussel, preferring the advice of her courtiers. They alleged that Gondi deliberately exaggerated the situation. Far from quelling the riot, he had clearly encouraged it. He had even been seen blessing the rioters! The decision was therefore taken to stand firm and to send Chancellor Seguier next morning to the Palais de Justice to forbid the *Parlement* to debate further the arrest of their leaders.

But the unpopular Seguier never reached the Palais de Justice. As soon as he poked his nose out into the streets he was set upon by an armed mob and had to dive into the first unlocked door he could find. He trembled in a cellar while the mob sacked the house. Seguier would only emerge when a rescue party arrived headed by Marshal de la Meilleraie. Next day, all the householder's possessions were returned to him undamaged - proof of the mob's idealism. Seguier had got nowhere and the barricades remained.

The *Parlement* continued to confer. Its members decided that they should all proceed to the Palais Royal to petition for Broussel's release. President Molé was to be their spokesman. Initially he was no more successful than Gondi. But Henrietta Maria, profiting from her English experience, persuaded Anne to listen. After Molé had spoken, the regent replied that she would only release Broussel if *Parlement* promised not to meddle. This the magistrates were reluctant to concede, but further mob violence persuaded both sides to compromise. On the evening of 27 August, Broussel, still wearing his slippers, returned home in triumph. Sanity, it seemed, had prevailed. But not for long. Both sides manoeuvred for position, while tension rose. Paris was flooded with scurrilous pamphlets - the famous *Mazarinades* - which attacked and ridiculed the queen and her chief minister.

> I don't blame the cardinal, he's just a foreigner out for revenge.
> I forgive him. But I'd like to strangle our whore of a queen

Mazarin's inability to pronounce French properly was the least of the crimes of which he was accused. Most of these jingles speculated about Mazarin's greed, lechery and low birth ('un étranger de très sordide naissance'). While Italians had a reputation for vice, Sicilians were thought to be even worse. So it was alleged - wrongly - that Mazarin was

Sicilian. However the Mazarinades may have been right when they implied a sexual relationship between regent and chief minister. It is less probable that Mazarin was Louis XIV's father - or his lover! But damage was done. Mazarin remarked bitterly that his nieces were now his daughters. Meanwhile the *Parlement* revived a law of 1617 which banned foreigners from office. Mazarin was equated with Concini.

On 22 October the government issued the declaration of Saint Germain, which accepted the Chambre Saint Louis programme. This declaration was registered by the *Parlement* two days later, the same date on which the Peace of Westphalia was signed. Mazarin's comment is understandable:

> You must admit that it requires a commitment to the very limit and a quite extraordinary zeal to redouble one's efforts in public service - as I do - when one is treated so badly and at a time when it would seem possible to say without vanity that my efforts are beginning to bear fruit.

In fact, both sides were preparing for war. The regent and her chief minister took the court to Saint Germain (twenty miles outside Paris) and prepared to attack the capital. Condé, the victor of Rocroi and Lens, was recruited for triumphs against his own countrymen. Nor had the *parlementaires* been idle. They suspected that the declaration of Saint Germain was dust in the eye and would be repudiated. On 8 January 1649 they decreed Mazarin's banishment as a 'disturber of public tranquility'. Noblemen such as Beaufort and Conti, Condé's hunch-backed brother, offered their swords to the magistrates, while Gondi the Coadjutator co-ordinated resistance with the *parlements* of Rouen and Aix, both capitals of discontented provinces.

War broke out at the end of January when the royal army led by Condé besieged Paris. It was a squalid affair in which there was much hardship in the city, though little fighting. Condé captured the important outpost of Charenton from his brother, but he had little enthusiasm for 'this war of gutters and chamber-pots'. He was opposed not only by Conti and Beaufort but by Gondi the saint who raised a troop from the citizens of Paris, believing that his military equalled his political skills. There was amusement at court when his recruits ran away. However, the news that Turenne was returning from Germany to fight for the rebels and that the Parisians had contacted the Spaniards alarmed the regent. On the *Parlement's* side Molé favoured compromise. He and Mazarin's secretary of state Le Tellier negotiated the peace of Rueil (12 March 1649).

This was on the face of it a sensible compromise. The government confirmed the declaration of Saint Germain while the *Parlement* withdrew its measures directed at the chief minister. The nobles who had fought for the *Parlement* and who expected promotions to be extracted from the regent were indignant. Beaufort wanted to be governor of Brittany, Bouillon wanted Sedan back (taken from him after his involvement in the Cinq-Mars conspiracy) and Conti wanted the disgraced trouble-maker Madame de Chevreuse back. They had been betrayed! Molé also faced criticism from hard-line colleagues in the *Parlement.* But there was relief in Paris that the war was over. On 18 August 1649 Louis XIV returned to his capital, receiving a rapturous welcome from his loyal Parisians.

At this stage it is right to stress the achievements of the *Parlement de Paris.* Doubtless the magistrates' motives were mixed, their ideals outweighed by selfish considerations. Yet they had successfully campaigned for the rights of the subject against a tyrannical regime. During the siege of Paris they had literally stood by their guns. Yet they had displayed moderation throughout. Lloyd Moote writes that 'the parlementary Fronde was not entirely legal, but it certainly was legalistic'. This legalistic concern for precedent and correct procedure saved the *parlementaires* from extremist actions which would indeed have branded them as rebels. French people were well aware of what was happening on the other side of the Channel. Nothing distressed the magistrates more than Anne's accusation that they were republicans - a charge which their own moderation disproved. Far from wishing to execute Louis XIV, as Charles I had been, they wanted to preserve the crown from its critics by eradicating abuses. Molé's readiness to abandon his aristocratic allies sprang from awareness of the fate of the English crown and the English parliamentarians once the military had seized control. Avoiding the extremes of compliance with an authoritarian government on the one hand and radical revolution on the other, the magistrates played a weak hand well.

Should not Mazarin have welcomed the peace of Rueil for which he too could claim some credit? In a year's time the situation would be transformed when Louis XIV came of age. The young king would be able to disavow all concessions extracted by force from his mother when she was regent. And no doubt he would continue to be guided by his faithful chief minister. Why not simply accept peace and play for time? But that was not the option Mazarin now chose. Within a few weeks of the court's return to Paris he decided to raise the stakes, and as a result France was plunged into a far more damaging civil war.

c) The Aristocratic Fronde (January 1650 - February 1653)

Mazarin was neither a fool nor a warmonger. While it was indeed a tragedy that the Peace of Reuil did not last, in fairness we must establish why the chief minister chose such a high-risk strategy.

Unfortunately, the Peace of Reuil brought neither contentment nor stability. Lawlessness raged throughout France, for the defiance of the Parisian magistrates triggered off a series of protest movements against an unpopular regime. Confrontation occurred in Guyenne between the governor and the local magistrates. The sovereign courts in Normandy defied the government's tax-farmers. In Dauphiné royalist troops were expelled. Civil war broke out in Provence between governor Alais and the *Parlement* of Aix. As the government's credibility sank, it became impossible to raise taxation. Mazarin used up his last resources on a campaign on the northern frontier, gambling on quick victory. But neither Turenne nor Condé would fight for him, so the French offensive became a fiasco. Meanwhile unpaid royal troops looted, raped and murdered in the countryside around Paris, competing with the Fronde's army. Fifteen thousand people abandoned their homes and fled into the capital while parish registers reveal that about a quarter of the population in villages around Paris perished during the Fronde.

The situation inside Paris remained highly volatile. It was a great pity that Mazarin did not bring the king back as soon as peace was concluded, for the court's presence provided a guarantee of stability and brought trade for merchants and work for artisans. In the event, troublemakers had every opportunity to foment the fear which was such a feature of the Fronde - fear of starvation and disease, but above all of soldiers. Vilification of Mazarin plumbed new depths. One pamphlet, entitled *Le Custode du lit de la reine, qui dit tout* (the guard at the queen's bed who tells all) began: 'People don't doubt it any longer, it's true that he shags her'. When the government sentenced the author to be hanged, a mob rescued him from the scaffold. In this atmosphere of hatred and mistrust disappointed Frondeur nobles had a field-day. When Beaufort heard his generalship derided by royalist nobles in a café he pulled table-cloth and plates to the floor and a riot ensued. The queen wanted to prosecute Beaufort, but *Parlement* assured her that she had no chance of getting a verdict against the 'king of the markets'. On 11 December 1649 Gondi's secretary, Guy Joly, survived an apparent assassination attempt, although it later transpired that his wounds had been self-inflicted in an attempt to drum up sympathy for his master. It was also alleged that there was a *Frondeur* plot to murder Condé.

In these circumstances Anne and Mazarin had two alternatives. They could form a coalition government, winning over the *Frondeurs* with the high office that they coveted and Condé's faction with military commands and provincial governorships. But the queen loathed Beaufort and Gondi, while Condé resented the 'ingratitude' with which he had been treated after the siege of Paris. At the best of times he was a difficult man, but now his arrogance and greed for power made him impossible. So Mazarin opted for the second alternative - which, in any case, was more to his taste - to play the rival factions off against each other. His first inclination was to support Condé against the Frondeurs by prosecuting them for attempting his murder. But the *Parlement* would not co-operate, the evidence being so nebulous. So Mazarin decided to ally with the Frondeurs and crush Condé.

After a secret pact had been negotiated with Gaston of Orleans and the Frondeurs, on 18 January 1650 Mazarin arrested Condé, his brother (Conti), and his brother-in-law (Longueville). The charge was treason. The three princes were imprisoned, first at Vincennes and then at Le Havre. Mazarin intended to follow up this coup by defeating Condé's armies and capturing his provincial strongholds. He hoped that this display of authority would restore the regime's credibility and overawe its enemies.

Was this a master-stroke or a mistake? Recent historians have argued that Mazarin had to proceed against Condé if he wished to remain chief minister. Orest Ranum writes: 'It was either arrest the princes or totally capitulate to Condé and give him control of the Council of State and the power to appoint governors'. But Mazarin had surely got it wrong again. Despite his political skills he did not understand the French. Perversely the *Parlement* of Paris took Condé's part, arguing that his detention conflicted with the terms of the Peace of Reuil which guaranteed the individual's freedom from unjustified imprisonment. As the regent could provide no evidence of Condé's treason, he should not be in prison. As a result, public opinion, exacerbated by xenophobia and snobbery, condemned the regent and her cardinal. What did this foreign woman and her jumped-up Italian boy-friend think they were doing, arresting the first prince of the blood? As Molé put it to Anne: 'Ah Madame, what have you done? These are children of the royal house.'

Mazarin soon found that he had overreached himself. He knew that he would have a fight on his hands. But he cannot have expected the bloody conflict which rapidly spread across France. While Condé enjoyed a lazy existence in prison, reading history and watering his plants, his supporters scattered to their strongholds and organised armed protest on his behalf. Condé exercised vast powers of patronage. People who lived on his estates, garrison commanders in the provinces which he controlled, clergy who owed their promotions to him, magistrates and lesser officials who were his creatures - all rallied to his cause. It was a most impressive demonstration of the patron-client relationship. Self-interest combined with obligation. And while nobody liked Condé, they disliked Mazarin even more. Temporarily at least, Condé was not only the patron to be supported in his hour of need. He was also a martyr to the Italian's tyranny.

Mazarin's plan was to place the overall conduct of policy in the hands of Gaston, the inexperienced Le Tellier, and the ex-frondeur Chateauneuf, who replaced an indignant Seguier as chancellor. This ill-assorted team was supposed to hold the fort in Paris while the boy-king, the queen-regent and the chief minister toured France, dealing with rebellion and drumming up support. Actually this was not a bad strategy. The medieval regionalism which was still such a feature of French political life made it hard to mount a national protest movement. To tour the realm picking off local rebellions before they could be co-ordinated therfore made sense. But Mazarin had too many enemies, and Condé too many sympathisers, including his old rival Turenne who was in love with Condé's sister, the duchess of Longueville. Condé's system of patronage was more effective than Mazarin's. While Mazarin certainly had his creatures in strategic positions, Condé commanded the unquestioning obedience of whole provinces. For example, in Guyenne his supporters combined with the *Parlement* of Bordeaux against Epernon, the royalist governor.

Ironically it was the chief minister's successes which brought about his downfall. Having pacified Bordeaux, Mazarin led the royal army to victory at Rethel against Turenne and the Spanish (14 December 1650). Gaston was jealous and the *Parlement* alarmed, remembering the cardinal's reactions to the victory at Lens. Would further arrests now follow? In an undignified quarrel, Mazarin accused Gaston of causing the downfall of the monarchy, comparing him to Fairfax and Cromwell. Gaston replied that Mazarin was off his head. Gondi's memoirs tell how Gaston whistled through his teeth when about to walk away from a decision. But now with uncharacteristic decisiveness Gaston teamed up with Gondi and Molé. The *Parlement* was encouraged to petition the regent both for the release of the princes and for the dismissal of the hated Italian. Mazarin capitulated. After an abortive discussion with Condé at Le Havre he slunk away into exile at Cologne (February 1651). The princes returned to Paris in triumph. Meanwhile Gondi heard that the regent was about to remove the king from Paris. So he surrounded the Palais-Royal with troops while crowds of Parisians filed through the king's bedroom to assure themselves that he was still there. Louis feigned sleep while Anne watched in impotent rage.

There now followed months of anarchy. The queen regent, without her beloved chief minister's support, was out of her depth. Mazarin continued to counsel her, but not even he could achieve government by correspondence, for his advice was usually out of date by the time it arrived. Anne would have been wiser to have listened to Le Tellier who was on the spot and no fool. It is impossible not to sympathise with her:

> I no longer know when to expect your return, since every day brings obstacles to prevent it. All I can say is that I am very upset about it and bear this delay with great impatience; and if sixteen [Mazarin] knew all that fifteen [Anne] suffers on that account, I feel sure that he would be touched. I have received your letters almost every day, and without that I do not know what would happen. Continue to write to me as often since you console me in the state in which I am.

Two *Mazarinades* indicate the sympathy Anne could expect in Paris:

> Here we have a bitch, dressed up in cardinal's robes.
>
> You can see the original by studying the copy.

If he comes back, whatever shall we do? We could cut off his private parts. But the king says: 'Don't do that, Mama still has a use for them'.

Meanwhile problems proliferated. Condé behaved insufferably, he insisted on replacing Epernon as governor of Guyenne and quarrelled with everyone, including Turenne who had been prevailed upon to take over command of the royal armies. He also alienated Gondi who had been bribed with a cardinal's hat to join the government. As he was now Cardinal de Retz surely he would achieve his goal and become chief minister. But it was not to be. The young king came of age on 7 September 1651. A few weeks later he recalled his godfather from exile. Mazarin returned with a body-guard of 6,000 German mercenaries. On 23 March 1652 the *Parlement* isssued Remonstrances to Louis XIV:

Cardinal Mazarin has shown, by seeking to continue the war, that he does not care about the future: he has employed all his efforts in this, exhausting the supplies of soldiers and money in France. We now see that he has caused such disorder that we are in both a foreign and a civil war. Who can doubt that Cardinal Mazarin wanted to have the sole direction of the war? When Cardinal Mazarin considers what happened over thirty years ago to a person of his nation, who was much less criminal than himself, he will judge the danger into which he has fallen.

Mazarin was terrified by comparisons between himself and Concini, well aware that his fellow-Italian had been assassinated. Fortunately for him, Condé came to the government's rescue by alienating everyone. The prince excelled himself by committing war-crimes in Paris. Having failed to dominate Bordeaux, he raided the capital. But in suffocating heat he was beaten outside the walls near the Faubourg Saint-Antoine by Turenne. 'I have lost all my friends', Condé complained after the battle, as he stripped naked in a field to cool off. However, he gained admission to the city due to a lady's intervention. While Gaston could not decide whom to support, his daughter turned the Bastille's guns on Turenne's victorious army - one of the many occasions during the Fronde when women influenced events. Troops ran amok in the streets of Paris, set houses on fire and massacred magistrates when Condé made a clumsy attempt to bully the *Parlement*. When a priest tried to put out the fires and prevent the massacre by producing a miraculous host (the consecrated bread offered at Mass), Condé's troops knocked him down and 'committed violences on him unworthy of Christians and Catholics'. Condé set up a puppet regime under Broussel and Beaufort. But Broussel was too old, Beaufort had an argument with his brother-in-law Nemours and killed him in the inevitable duel, while Condé quarrelled with everyone, including Gaston and the citizens of

Paris. A few weeks later he left France to serve the King of Spain. He was finished.

Mazarin meanwhile voluntarily went into exile again, lest his presence alienate support from the government. Louis XIV was thus able to make an uncontested entry into Paris on 21 October 1652. *Parlement* and government co-operated over a general amnesty, although ten magistrates including Broussel were banished to the provinces. Gaston was welcomed back - again. To his bewilderment Cardinal de Retz was sent to prison. Mazarin returned to Paris in February 1653.

Does anyone emerge from the Princes' Fronde with credit? Mazarin? He displayed flexibility, but he provoked the Fronde and was ultimately saved only by luck, his status as a cardinal, and the devotion of Anne of Austria. Furthermore he was not the disinterested patriot of French historiography. His quarrel with Condé was over such matters as patronage and the promotion of his own family just as much as over policy and principles. The nobles? Did not the selfishness and irresponsibility of Condé, Beaufort, de Retz and others fully justify the authoritarian rule of Louis XIV? Richard Bonney has argued that the nobles deserve respect for having a programme: Richelieu's administrative revolution to be cancelled, the *intendants* to go, taxes to be reduced, peace to be urgently sought with Spain, and the princes of the blood to replace the foreign adventurer at the centre of government. These were the goals of most conservative, aristocratic Frenchmen, though whether they transcend mere reactionary selfishness is open to dispute. The way that the participants changed sides so often hardly inspires confidence in their devotion to principle. Indeed Mazarin's departures into exile revealed that really there was only one unifying 'principle' - hatred of Mazarin.

Interesting light is thrown on the nobles' motivation by de Retz's memoirs, for he stresses not only his own scandalously unrecognised ability but also his aristocratic principles. For instance, he claims that as an aristocrat he was above worldly ambition, he had no wish to be made a cardinal, and only wanted to be chief minister for the sake of France, for it was in France's interests that true nobles should wield power. Understandably his bête-noir was Mazarin. How could it be right that this low-born foreigner should exclude nobles such as himself? With his stress on style and appearances de Retz personified the aristocratic code. He prided himself on his own honourable conduct, truthfulness, indifference to money, physical courage. How unlike the deceitful Sicilian! It is significant that de Retz was ambivalent towards Condé. Though like everyone else he found the great general incomprehensible, he nevertheless desperately looked for hidden virtues. Given Condé's high birth, the virtues must be there! One is reminded of Robin Briggs's observation: 'The maintenance of unreasonable demands could be almost synonymous with the status of a grandee'.

Ultimately even the most unreasonable nobles agreed with

magistrates, churchmen, merchants and peasants that an ordered state ruled by an unpopular chief minister was preferable to disorder. And if there had to be war, Frenchmen might as well fight Spaniards rather than each other. Even the Frondeurs were eventually sickened by the Fronde.

d) The Fronde in Bordeaux - the *Ormée* (1652-3)

To find radical policies and genuine idealism during the Fronde we must look to Bordeaux. Here the *Ormée* occurred. We have seen how uneven the opposition to the crown was in provincial France. Aix, for example, was perpetually seething with disaffection, whereas Lyon, the second largest city of the realm, remained loyal. Bordeaux had a long history of subversion and defiance. Epernon, the royal governor of Guyenne, was detested. Bordeaux's citizens were electrified by the reports from Paris during the *Fronde Parlementaire.* Conflict between the city and the governor was exacerbated by the arrival of Condé's wife and child in May 1650, shortly after her husband's imprisonment. Stalemate led to a visit by Anne of Austria and the boy king in September 1650. But Condé's nomination as governor of Guyenne (May 1651) in place of Epernon raised the expectations of the radicals.

However, Bordeaux was divided against itself. The chief executive authority was the *jurade* or town council, dominated by rich bourgeois. The chief judicial authority was the *parlement* dominated by the magistrates of the robe nobility. They were at daggers drawn. Both Mazarin and Condé exploited patronage in order to play off *parlement* and *jurade* against each other. As a result, the situation was confused. It was against this background that the *Ormée* emerged in 1652. It was a radical party composed of *petits bourgeois* and artisans. Its members met under the elm trees in the city centre, hence their name (*orme* means elm). They hated both Mazarin and Epernon, and were impatient with the timidity of both *parlement* and *jurade.* When ordered to discontinue their meetings, they refused. They were led by Christophe Dureteste, a prosperous lawyer and a man of intelligence, idealism and initiative.

In June 1652 blood flowed when the *Ormée* stormed the *Chapeau Rouge* (the part of the city inhabited by the wealthy bourgeoisie) and seized power. Dureteste tried to put into practice the Ormist manifesto which was based on two Latin quotations: *'Vox populi vox Dei'* ('The voice of the people is the voice of God') and *'Estote prudentes sicut serpentes et simplices sicut colombae'* ('Be ye therefore wise as serpents and harmless as doves'). No one was to be victimised on account of rank, which meant that the upper classes lost their monopoly of power:

> 1 The restoration of the French state can only be accomplished by the people. The great nobles and magistrates are the accomplices

> and disciples of tyranny; if the people turn to other military leaders than those who are among them, in order to free themselves, they will prolong their hardship.

This was fighting talk, and the *Ormée* leadership was prepared to fight in order to retain power. Strong-armed squads representing the council of thirty, the *Ormée's* executive, visited recalcitrant noblemen. Dureteste conveyed this message to one such aristocrat:

> Having learnt that you are ill, I am bringing you an order that you are to take some fresh air. And if in twenty-four hours you have not departed, you will be murdered and thrown into the river.

The Articles of Union which the *Ormée* regime now published continued to stress the role of Christian love in a Christian society, the importance of taxation fairly assessed and collected, the provision of health care for the destitute, and a promise to look after widows and orphans. The regime did its best for the 'menu peuple' (the 'little people') who seldom counted for much in the hard-hearted seventeenth-century world. At first the leaders of the *Ormée* protested their loyalty to the king and it was only in the later stages that republican sentiments were expressed. Perhaps this was a result of a visit from the Leveller Edward Sexby who brought the English revolutionaries' manifesto the *Agreement of the People* to Bordeaux.

But time was running out for the *Ormée*. 'The people are howling for bread and peace', Dureteste was told. Due to the collapse of the wine and grain trades, the city was starving and terrorised by gangs of youths who were beyond the administration's control. A desperate appeal for help was sent to Cromwell, but in vain. In July 1653 Mazarin intrigued with the Bordeaux *parlementaires,* and the *Ormée* collapsed when royal troops appeared before the town. Dureteste went into hiding but was betrayed in January 1654. He was tried by the *Parlement,* broken on the wheel in the presence of his erstwhile supporters, and then executed under the elm trees where his remarkable and courageous experiment in social justice had begun. There had also been brief, flickering protests by the poor against the rich in Paris, Rouen and Aix. But only the leaders of the *Ormée* actually seized power - at the time a unique achievement unparalleled in either England or France.

e) The Last Years of Cardinal Mazarin (1653-61)

Cardinal Mazarin's last years as ruler of France were fraught with difficulties, for the problems which had caused the Fronde remained unsolved. Given that the ruinously costly war against Spain continued, it might be thought that Mazarin would have learned from experience and introduced financial reform. Not so, however. He exploited his victory over the *Frondeurs* by reintroducing the old, corrupt system. His only concession was to do so bit-by-bit. During the Fronde the office-holders whose responsibility it was to raise taxes - the *élus* and *trésoriers* - had temporarily recovered their influence at the expense of the hated *intendants.* Now they promised Mazarin that if they were allowed to continue they would ensure that the crown received its due. But Mazarin rejected their offers and soon the *intendants* were being introduced spasmodically, often styled *maîtres des requests* which was less provocative. The financiers were back in business as well, once again making vast fortunes at the taxpayers' expense. To administer this racket Mazarin appointed three superintendants of finance on the assumption that the cleverest and crookedest would outsmart the others, thus proving his merit. So it turned out. Indeed during the cardinal's last years Nicolas Fouquet turned corruption into an art form. His palace, Vaux-le-Vicomte, stands as a monument to his taste.

The rivival of 'fiscal terrorism' provoked predictably bitter reactions. As it happened the 1650s were years of poor harvests and widespread plague. Therefore the taxman was especially unwelcome. Peasant revolts flared up throughout France. Typical of these were the *sabotiers* (clog-wearers) who disrupted the countryside south of Orleans in 1658. The nobles were disaffected, rebelling in nine provinces between 1657 and 1659. The towns defied the government. For example, in 1656 Angers had to be occupied by a royal army, and Louis XIV and Mazarin invaded Provence in January 1660, treating Marseille like a conquered city.

Paris continued to give the government trouble, though it was trouble of a bizarre kind. The parish clergy decided to take on Cardinal Mazarin in what some historians have dubbed 'the Religious Fronde'. Their figurehead was de Retz, now not only a cardinal but, since his uncle's death in July 1654, Archbishop of Paris as well - for a coadjutor automatically succeeded when his bishop died. However, de Retz was an absentee archbishop. He had escaped into exile by climbing down the castle wall at Nantes, though unfortunately he fell off his getaway horse and dislocated his shoulder (one of the most profound turning-points in history, de Retz assures us in his memoirs). The clergy of Paris defied the government's attempts to replace de Retz with a reliable yes-man, nor would the pope depose de Retz even though Mazarin pointed out that his fellow-cardinal was an atheist. The clergy were motivated by loyalty to their archbishop, hatred of Mazarin, and concern for the victims of high taxation. They were also affected by two religious movements. Jansenism was a kind of Roman Catholic puritanism which was a reaction against the allegedly permissive, morally lax Jesuits whose influence at court was especially distrusted, while Richerism championed the rights of parish priests to be free from papal and episcopal interference.

The government found it difficult to counter this protest movement which the clergy conducted with eloquence from their pulpits. Public opinion rallied to the clergy, adopting their leader Père Chassebras as a cult-figure. The government was aware that strong-arm tactics would create martyrs. But in any case they could neither capture de Retz the figurehead who was hundreds of miles away and refused to resign his archbishopric, nor locate Chassebras who hid in the tower of Saint Jean-en-Crève. Furthermore, Chassebras had a printing-press up there in his tower from which Paris was flooded with anti-government pamphlets and Mazarinades. Chancellor Seguier was at his wits' end. Over two thirds of Paris clergy were involved in this defiance and the government was made to look ridiculous. The revolt of the curés only ended when Mazarin died and when de Retz was finally persuaded to resign as archbishop. Louis XIV ordered him to Rome to represent French interests - a top job at last! He hated it.

Mazarin sought relief from these problems by concentrating on more congenial tasks. The first was the training of the young king. Nature had been kind to Louis XIV. He was intelligent, charming, handsome and healthy. His appetites were relatively harmless - until he fell in love with one of Mazarin's nieces. Mazarin wanted his nieces to marry well, but not that well! After wobbling miserably for several weeks, Louis did as he was told and ended the relationship. He also followed his godfather's advice in matters of state. He was the perfect pupil and Mazarin was understandably proud of him. 'God has given you every gift including deceitfulness', he perceptively remarked to his monarch. 'All you have to do is use your gifts and you will be a great king'. Louis, Mazarin and Anne were a close-knit trio. Louis acquired his mother's unthinking piety and his god-father's cynicism.

The other task to which Mazarin now gave attention was the re-creation of his own fortune, for during the Fronde he had lost everything. The *Parlement* of Paris had even sold off his library. But now the cardinal seized the opportunity to retrieve the situation. During the last eight years of his life he acquired an immense fortune. Given that a wealthy nobleman might amass seven or eight million livres, and that Richelieu's fortune of 22 million was considered to be exceptional, the fact that Mazarin left 37 million is remarkable. Pictures, jewels, estates, bishoprics and cash were accumulated by the old miser. His man of business was Jean-Baptiste Colbert who never missed a trick, whether it was a matter of noting the corruption of Nicolas Fouquet the superintendant of finance whose job he coveted or of increasing his master's wealth. Shortly before he died Mazarin gave his whole fortune to the king, calculating that this generous gesture would be refused. Louis left Mazarin in agonised suspense for twenty-four hours before returning the present. All had come right for the old gambler in the end.

Politically Cardinal Mazarin's achievements were no less remarkable. While there was still much for Louis XIV to do if France was to become prosperous and stable, nevertheless Mazarin had re-established the machinery of authoritarian rule. The *intendants* again fulfilled their dual role as tax-collectors and suppressors of opposition. The alliance between the crown and the political nation, especially the office-holders, had been restored. The nobles' claims to provincial governorships and independent commands had been contained. Royal patronage was again functioning smoothly. Condé had made his peace, while Le Tellier was busy creating a truly royal army, free from aristocratic domination. Although Mazarin lacked Richelieu's world-wide vision, France's frontiers were more secure. Due to the peace treaties which Mazarin had helped to negotiate France now dominated Europe while the king's marriage to the Spanish infanta would bring even more dazzling prospects. By his own lights Mazarin served France and its ruling dynasty effectively.

Of course one can question Mazarin's priorities and achievements, just as it can be argued that Richelieu was not necessarily 'France's greatest public servant'. There is no evidence that Mazarin regretted the glaring social and economic anomalies and injustices of Bourbon France. He did nothing for French industry or agriculture. The taxation system remained scandalously inefficient and corrupt. The government was now burdened by sixty thousand office holders. Mazarin complacently accepted the crown's crippling debts while he made his own fortune. But perhaps the most serious charge that could be laid against him is that he bequeathed his apparent unawareness of the true needs of the French people to his royal pupil. The Sun King with all his strengths as a politician and a monarch remained a conservative and uninspired initiator of policy. Here he was true to his guide and mentor, the cardinal.

What of Mazarin himself? He had inherited vast problems which were made worse by his own errors and by French xenophobia. Yet he learnt from his mistakes and seldom lost his nerve or his keen sense of the possible. Despite the abuse heaped on him, Mazarin was seldom vindictive in his treatment of others. He may have murdered the French language, but unlike Richelieu he did not murder Frenchmen. Among the enemies whom he imprisoned, perhaps de Retz was harshly treated - though there had been provocation. No doubt Mazarin had much to answer for. He was corrupted by power and his greed was unattractive. He was an ambitious dynast, preoccupied with marrying his nieces to the rich and powerful. When Hortensia married La Meilleraye's son, Mazarin arranged for him to receive the title duc de Mazarin! Nevertheless, while Mazarin may have been an acqusitive worldling, he was a civilised man whom it is hard to dislike. His dying words were touching and humble: 'The hour of mercy, the hour of mercy'.

f) The Fronde - an Evaluation

Now that we have surveyed the causes, course and consequences of the

Fronde, we can examine its nature and its significance. How do we evaluate this dramatic crisis which tore France apart for five long years? Was the Fronde a genuine revolution? Was it constructive or sterile? Was it, as some historians have argued, part of a greater, mid-seventeenth-century crisis, involving confrontations between rulers and ruled throughout Europe? Or do events in other countries pinpoint contrasts rather than parallels? In particular what light is thrown by comparison with the Great Rebellion in contemporary England?

First, are we dealing with a revolution when we examine the Fronde? Some historians think so. The subtitle of Orest Ranum's book on the Fronde is 'A French Revolution'. Louis Madelin called the Fronde *'une révolution manquée'* - a revolution that failed. On the other hand, as we have seen, Goubert in his biography of Mazarin argues that you have to cross the Channel to find a real revolution.

If we take revolution to mean 'forcible overthrow of a political system' or 'radical change of circumstance' *(Penguin English Dictionary)*, Ranum has a case. While Mazarin was the first to appeal to violence, the Paris magistrates quickly organised their own armed forces in defence of their political reforms. Still more did the princes resort to force in their attempts to overthrow the system of government founded by Richelieu. As for radical change the leaders of the *Fronde Parlementaire* forced the government to accept the *Chambe Saint Louis* programme. For example, the *intendants* were scrapped. This was no mean achievement, however insincere the government may have been. Similarly the noble Frondeurs were successful in chasing out Cardinal Mazarin - twice. He was replaced by Condé and de Retz. If these appointments had proved permanent, the nobles would have re-established their supremacy in the royal council and Richelieu's system would have been forcibly overthrown and radically changed.

On the other hand, these changes look much less radical when we examine them closely. The *Chambe Saint Louis* programme was cautious and conservative, reflecting the hitherto accepted rights of upper-class Frenchmen. This programme has been compared to the reforms of the Long Parliament. But the contrast here is striking. The removal of the prerogative courts and the Triennial Act in England were more sweeping than the proposals of the Paris magistrates. Even less impressive are the changes achieved by the princes. This was surely a matter of 'outs' replacing 'ins'. There was no question of the system being changed, simply a row about who exploited the system. This was not revolution.

When we compare what actually happened on the two sides of the Channel the contrasts look even sharper. It is not so much a matter of the 'selfishness' of the *Frondeurs,* for the English opponents of Charles I were 'selfish' too. As Christopher Hill has argued, 'liberty' usually meant 'privilege'. What matters is that irrespective of people's motives Stuart England really was turned upsidedown. The king was executed, the House of Lords was abolished and a military dictatorship was established. The upper classes were replaced both in national and local government by new men of little or no social standing. The control of the Church of England over the nation's spiritual and intellectual development was smashed. The governing classes in church and state got the fright of their lives. Now that was revolution! In France on the other hand the unpleasant, violent disruption of society between 1648 and 1653 was basically superficial rather than radical or unprecedented, for that sort of thing had being happening since the wars of religion in the sixteenth century. It was only too familiar a feature of the French way of life. In other words, we do not have a 'radical change of circumstances'.

Can one go further and argue that whereas the English revolutionaries succeeded the French failed? In a real sense both 'revolutions' failed. In both England and France the establishments were restored and 'revolutionary' innovations were cancelled. 'Where is your good old cause now?' Major-General Harrison was asked as he was hustled to the scaffold in July 1660. Similarly in France the financiers and the *intendants* were soon restored and so was Mazarin. Broussel was exiled, de Retz was bundled off to Rome and Condé ended his days rowing ladies round the lake at Versailles. But you cannot wholly put the clock back and pretend that events have not happened. England was permanently transformed by her revolution. Similarly French people, from Louis XIV downwards, were certainly affected by their experience of the Fronde. Lloyd Moote maintains that Colbert, in particular, appreciated why the Fronde happened, hence his sweeping reforms of law and finance in the 1660s. Similarly, never again would the regime alienate the office-holders. Furthermore, not even Louis XIV at his most arbitrary would try to overrule the *Parlements'* rights to legislate - for instance, when he tried to establish the rights of his bastards to succeed to the throne. In other words, Moote claims that whether or not the Fronde was a revolution, it was not a failure.

But again we are back with contrasts. If there was indeed a general mid-seventeenth-century European crisis, each country was different and nowhere is this truism more apparent than when we examine the mid-century ructions in England and France. The most striking contrast is the clean sweep which the revolutionaries made in England, for between 1646 and 1660 they actually exercised power. As a result dynamic developments in trade, foreign policy, religion, political and scientific thought were the permanent legacy of the revolution. And even though the traditional governing class was restored in 1660, England progressed inexorably towards limited monarchy guaranteed by constitutional law. It is impossible to match these achievements when we analyse the Fronde. Compared to the English revolution it comes across as basically negative and sterile.

Why was this so? Mainly because the Frondeurs failed to defeat the crown. They never had the opportunity to put their ideas into practice nor the necessity to work out a realistic programme because they never fully took over the government. The English revolutionaries on the other hand defeated the crown and had to create a political alternative. They had to be positive rather than negative.

Why did the English revolutionaries win and the Frondeurs lose? This question brings us to the heart of our investigation into the nature of the Fronde. Superficially both English and French crises began in the same way. In both countries an unpopular regime faced bankruptcy due to involvement in an apparently unwinnable war. In both England and France ministers were pilloried. Both regimes made concessions followed by ill-advised attempts to arrest trouble-makers. But then the stories diverge. Charles I was a poor leader, lacking Anne of Austria's staunchness and Mazarin's realism and flexibility. The French crown had greater military and financial resources; its income was five times higher than England's, a point taken by money-lenders who were more willing to rescue Louis XIV than Charles I. The English crown alienated a coherent cross-section of the political nation. In France the sword and the robe nobility soon fell out and could be played off against each other by the crown. To co-ordinate and lead its varied factions every revolt needs a Lenin - or a Cromwell. No such leader emerged in France. Mazarin erred when he compared Condé with Fairfax and de Retz with Cromwell. As for external support, whereas the Scots rescued the English parliament, the Spanish played a minimal role in France.

Again, for a revolution to succeed in drastically altering the status quo it must, as Robin Briggs argues, target and destroy 'an identifiable, responsible adult goon'. Louis XVI, Nicholas II and above all Charles I filled this particular bill. Cardinal Mazarin did not, for a chief minister however detested is not ultimately responsible and can therefore be removed without bringing down the regime. Nor did Anne of Austria, for a regent's tenure of power will soon end. Nor did Louis XIV. You cannot attack a twelve year old boy, especially in a king-worshipping society and especially when the boy in question had Louis' poise and good looks ('not so much a puppet as a poppet king', as one historian has remarked). What else could the Frondeurs do but protest their loyalty to the crown?

Another vital contrast between England and France is that *parlement* did not equal Parliament. Granted, the prestige of the *Parlement* of Paris was considerable, as was that of the provincial *parlements.* But they were merely courts, fulfilling only narrow legal functions. By contrast the English Parliament, while a 'High Court' involved in creating statute law, was much more than that. It had consolidated its position as a deliberative and consultative assembly with the right to criticise the king's ministers and policies. True, it had not yet established the principle of ministerial responsibility to Parliament - but that was in the Grand Remonstrance (November 1641). Nor had it yet established the control of the sword - but that was in the Militia Ordinance (March 1642). Furthermore Parliament represented the English nation, in however ill-defined a way and however restricted the concept of nation. The magistrates in the *Parlement* of Paris represented no-one but themselves, for they had bought their positions and had not been elected. Their jurisdiction covered less than half of France. As Richard Bonney remarks, 'there were really four separate conflicts in 1649 based on the *Parlements* of Paris, Rouen, Aix and Bordeaux'. When they created provincial *parlements* the French kings knew what they were doing. In a very loose way the *Parlement* of Paris had become the mouthpiece of the nation's grievances during the early stages of the Fronde. But its position was indeterminate and unofficial. If any institution spoke for the whole nation, it was the Estates General which had not met since 1615 and was not to meet again until 1789. This lack of an organisation qualified to represent the nation gravely handicapped any opposition movement in France.

Religion provides the greatest contrast between the Fronde and the Great Rebellion. Puritanism inspired and justified Parliament's rebellion. The New Model Army's high morale and Cromwell's ruthless determination were likewise religious, while Royalists also believed that they did God's will. The role of religion in the Fronde by contrast was nil. We have seen that the Parisian *curés* were infected with Jansenism. But that was after the Fronde had ended. Nothing is more striking than the low profile adopted by the Huguenots. The *Ormée's* historian S.A. Westrich writes: 'The relations between the *Ormée* and Bordeaux's Huguenots is not very clear, but there can be little doubt that the latter supported the rebellion if only tacitly, and that the *Ormée* was well disposed towards them'. This is not impressive. How do you support a rebellion tacitly? Mazarin expressed his appreciation of the Huguenots' loyalty during the Fronde. Clearly, historians should agree with the cardinal that religion did not significantly affect the Fronde.

Every protest movement needs ideals. While people will risk their lives for personal gain, they will only fight for a cause if they believe in it. The cause does not have to be religious. It can, for example, represent country, class or race. But it has to convince the troops. In Cromwell's phrase, they must have 'the root of the matter in them'. Can one see any idealism in the Fronde? It is not a question of moral judgement. You may prefer Condé's brutality or de Retz's self-dramatisation to Cromwell's canting self-righteousness. But Cromwell believed in it, and so did his supporters. Two centuries later the artist Auguste Renoir was mistaken for a spy during the Commune because he was painting a picture. Subsequently he remarked of the Communards: 'They were madmen, but they had in them that little flame which never dies'. Molet's dry legalism and Condé's aristocratic code were unlikely to inspire anyone. The *Mazarinades* compare badly with 'God made them as stubble to our swords', 'In the name of the Commons in Parliament assembled and all the good people of England', 'We are not a mercenary army', and 'Jesus Christ is the Head Leveller'. Apart from the *Ormée* such ringing declarations are absent from the Fronde.

Yet there is a case for the Frondeurs. They were not wholly selfish or futile. In their inadequate, muddled way they challenged a system which many contemporaries thought tyrannical. Indeed the Fronde was the last serious protest against Bourbon authoritarianism before the French Revolution swept it away in a sea of bloodshed. Was its defeat entirely in the interests of the French people?

Chronological Summary of the Fronde

15 Jan	1648	*Lit de Justice.* New offices and taxes registered.
13 May	1648	Edict of Union. Courts to meet in Chambre Saint Louis.
9 Jul	1648	D'Emery replaced by La Meilleraie as Superintendant.
31 Jul	1648	*Lit de Justice.* Reform proposals provisionally accepted.
20 Aug	1648	Condé's victory at Lens.
26 Aug	1648	*Te Deum* at Notre Dame. Arrest of Broussel.
27 Aug	1648	Barricades. Broussel released.
24 Oct	1648	Government accepted reform programme.
6 Jan	1649	Court left Paris for Saint Germain.
8 Jan	1649	*Parlement* outlawed Mazarin.
Jan-Mar	1649	Siege of Paris.
8 Feb	1649	Condé captured Charenton.
12 Mar	1649	Treaty of Rueil. Reforms accepted, princes ignored.
11 Dec	1649	Assassination attempts against Joly and Condé.
18 Jan	1650	Mazarin arrested Condé, Conti and Longueville.
Jan 1650 - Feb 1653		Princes' Fronde.
Oct	1650	Louis XIV and Anne of Austria in Bordeaux.
14 Dec	1650	Battle of Rethel. Mazarin defeated Turenne.
8 Feb	1651	Mazarin released the princes at Le Havre and went into exile.
7 Sep	1651	Louis XIV came of age.
Dec	1651	Mazarin returned from exile.
Jun	1652	*Ormée* seized power in Bordeaux.
23 Mar	1652	*Parlement's* remonstances blamed Mazarin for the civil war.
2 Jul	1652	Battle of the Faubourg Saint Antoine.
4 Jul	1652	Massacre at the Hotel de Ville.
Jul	1652	Condé set up puppet government under Broussel and Beaufort.
Aug	1652	Mazarin's second exile.
Oct	1652	Condé left Paris and went into exile.
21 Oct	1652	Louis XIV returned to Paris.
Feb	1653	Mazarin returned from second exile.
20 Jul	1653	The *Ormée* defeated.

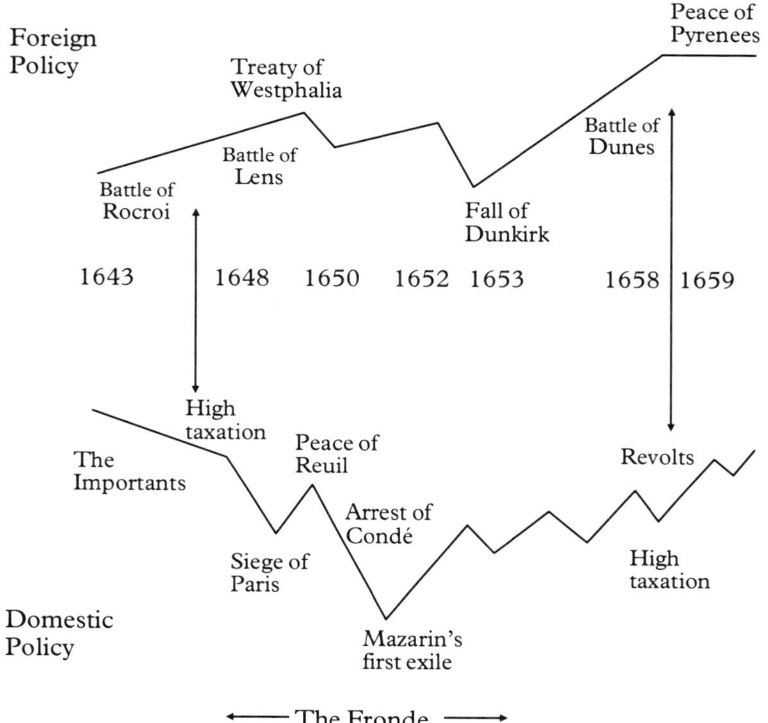

France's fortunes under Cardinal Mazarin

Making notes on *'The Ministry of Cardinal Mazarin'*

The Belgian historian Henri Pirenne wrote: 'Two dangers menace the discipline of history, the taste for easy work and the tendency to make history partisan'. You may well feel when studying the eighteen years of Cardinal Mazarin's ministry that partisanship is fairly easily avoided in that there are few characters with whom one can identify, but that 'the taste for easy work' is only too understandable. If only one could find basic principles and simple generalisations! But there are no short cuts. In finding your way through this morass efficient notes are essential.

Mazarin's foreign policy is a relatively straightforward topic. It would be prudent to make a detailed summary of the chronology of events and of the peace treaties of Westphalia and the Pyrenees. Make yourself familiar with the map on pages 123. Equip yourself with notes for the following questions:

1 Did Mazarin defend France's true interests in his conduct of foreign policy?
2 Why did it take so long to terminate the wars against the Habsburg powers?
3 How successful was Mazarin's foreign policy?

Making notes on the Fronde should provide you with a firm grasp of the story. First summarise the causes. Then work from the summary of events on page 118. If you do your job thoroughly, every event in that summary should be clear and meaningful to you. A possible approach would be to compile notes on the contributions of key figures: Anne of Austria, Mazarin, Condé, Gondi (de Retz), and Gaston. Make notes on such issues as the success or failure of the Fronde, the causes of its eventual collapse and the comparison with the English Revolution (especially if you have studied this topic). Make yourself familiar with the causes, course and collapse of the Ormée.

Answering essay questions on 'The Ministry of Cardinal Mazarin'

There is no reason why you should not be asked a question on Mazarin's foreign policy, but in the past examiners have tended to concentrate on the Fronde. It is also very possible that you will get a question requiring you to compare Richelieu and Mazarin. Although most examiners feel themselves unable to set questions asking for a comparison of the English and French revolts between 1642 and 1653, any marker worth her/his salt would give a candidate credit for perceptive cross-references.

Study the following questions:

1 Why was Mazarin able to survive the Frondes?
2 How successful was Mazarin's foreign policy?
3 What opposition did Mazarin encounter and why was he able to defy it?
4 How seriously was the French monarchy threatened by the Frondes?
5 With what justification can the Fronde be described as 'basically reactionary'?
6 'They achieved nothing because they aimed too high'. Discuss this assessment of the Frondeurs.
7 Is it reasonable to describe the Fronde as 'a revolution'?
8 Compare and contrast the achievements of Richelieu and Mazarin.

Questions about Mazarin's ability to survive are usually straightforward, though be careful to pay attention to the exact wording of the question.

It may or may not be solely about the Fronde. Questions about Mazarin's legacy to Louis XIV are quite common, but we will defer consideration of them until the end of the next chapter. Questions about the nature of the Fronde are often rather difficult. Let us consider question 4.

The technique of writing a good introduction is crucial here. Be sure to cover the following issues: What is the point of the question? Why is it a good question? You could begin by making the point that the Fronde revolts erupted at about the time when Charles I was being tried and executed. Frenchmen were well aware of this, indeed the Frondeurs were accused of republicanism by Mazarin's government. Historians, however, disagree as to the seriousness of the threat to the French crown.

In your development section demonstrate your appreciation of the question's complexity. In your first parargraph show that monarchy as such was consistently reverenced by the Frondeurs. Then you need a paragraph beginning 'But what sort of monarchy?' How radical would the changes to the French system of government have been if the Frondeurs had won? Show your familiarity with the Chambre Saint Louis programme and with the ambitions of Condé and Gondi (de Retz). You must then devote a paragraph to the issue of how close to success the Frondeurs came. Back up your argument with analysis of the key stages of the Fronde.

In your conclusion give a clear answer to the question. It is a good illustration of the topic's difficulty that a top class answer could just as well agree or disagree with the suggestion that the French monarchy was indeed seriously threatened! Mastery of the technique of writing a satisfactory conclusion will enable you to leave the reader in no doubt as to what you believe and why. Try to introduce the odd new point so that your conclusion is not mere recapitulation.

***Source-based questions on** 'The Ministry of Cardinal Mazarin'*

1 Mazarin and his Critics

Carefully read the protest of the *Trésuriers* (pages 97-8), the *Mazarinades* (pages 101, 102 and 104), *Parlement's* remonstrance (page 107), and Mazarin's comment on his treatment (page 102). Answer the following questions.

a) How reliable and how useful to the historian are the sources criticising Cardinal Mazarin? (6 marks)
b) Do these documents suggest that Mazarin was harshly judged by his contemporaries? Explain your answer. (4 marks).
c) What can be learned about the motives of the *frondeurs* from these sources. What other types of evidence can be used by historians when attempting to identify the *frondeurs'* motives? (10 marks)

CHAPTER 5

Conclusion: the Cardinals' Legacy to Louis XIV

On 10 March 1661 Louis XIV summoned his chief advisers in order to inform them who was to succeed Mazarin as chief minister. To everyone's surprise he nominated himself, and he was to fulfil the role for the next fifty-four years. At the very least this was an astonishing feat of endurance, and in fact the Sun King had many positive achievements to be proud of as well.

When he began this half-century of hard labour, what sort of inheritance did Louis XIV receive? Whereas it used to be thought that Cardinal Mazarin bequeathed his young master a strong hand, we now know that the reality was more complex. The old-fashioned picture of the 1650s will no longer suffice: the gracious queen, the wise old cardinal and the gifted young king presiding over a serene and contented nation. In truth these were stressful times, for life was tense and careworn both for Anne of Austria and her cardinal and for the French people. Granted, the forty years war against the Habsburgs was eventually concluded. But as a consequence of this war the crown was in debt to the tune of 451 million livres (according to Colbert's calculation), France was exhausted and the population was mutinous. Plague and famine were rife. As Louis XIV remarked in his memoirs, 'confusion reigned everywhere', for France was a land of social and political instability. Not being gifted with second sight, neither Anne nor Mazarin could have anticipated the Sun King's triumphs at home and abroad during the coming decades, for given the situation in 1661 such an outcome would have appeared improbable.

Nevertheless, this is not to deny that profound and significant changes had occurred in France during the half-century since the death of Henri IV. Our friend Rip van Winkle would have been impressed if he had gone to sleep in 1610 and awoken in 1661. Not that the appearance of France had altered significantly: still the Renaissance palaces and the imposing city walls contrasting with the urban slums and the peasants' hovels, still the disease-ridden people, the emaciated farm-animals. But the political landscape had changed significantly, and so had the intellectual and religious scene. Socially and economically too France was no longer the country she had been when the religious fanatic Ravaillac stabbed Henri IV.

While Louis XIV and his ministers faced great problems in 1661, potentially they were in a stronger position than their predecessors had been in 1610. Over the preceding half-century significant victories had been achieved against the forces of disruption. Time and again the nobles had been defeated, culminating in the failure of the aristocratic Fronde. Late-medieval bastard-feudalism had succumbed to the

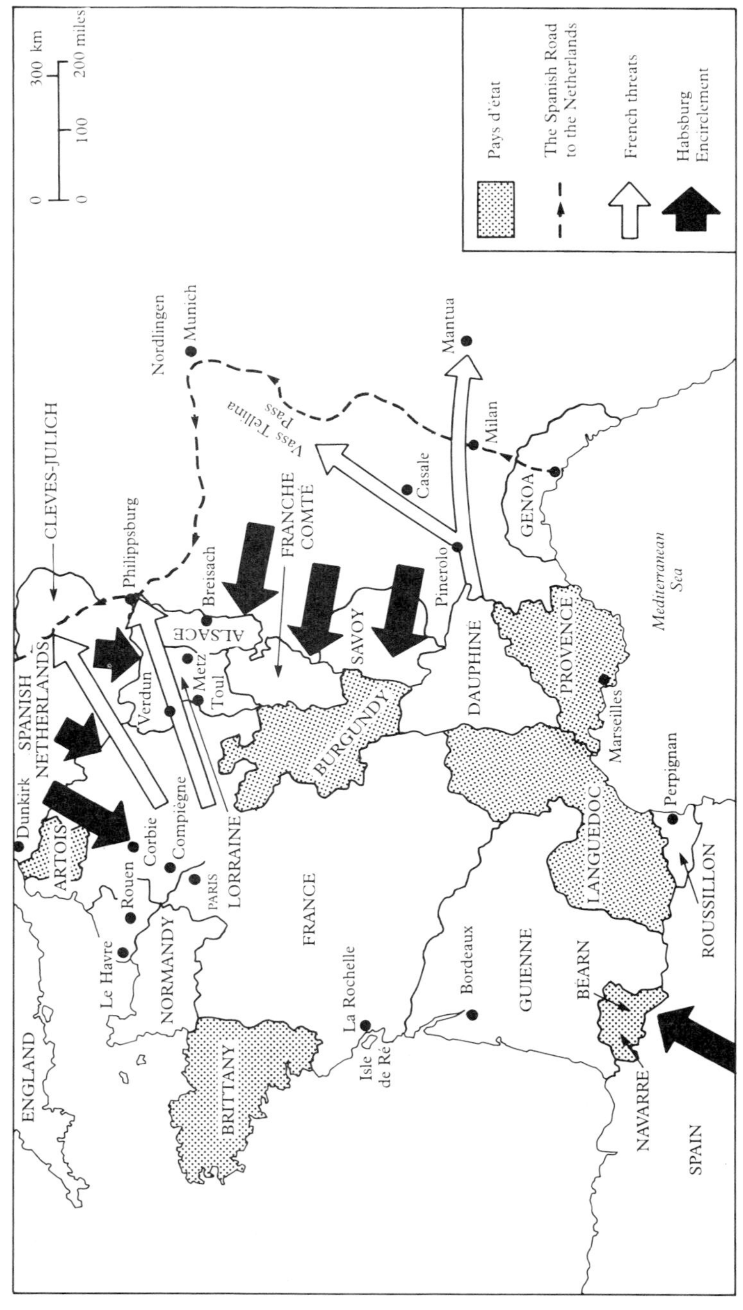

France in 1661

early-modern state. No longer could noblemen lead their own retainers or hijack royal armies against the crown. On the contrary, due to Le Tellier's reorganisation of the armed forces and especially of the structure of command in the field, the king now had what one historian has called a monopoly of violence. The Huguenots had displayed conspicuous loyalty during the Fronde, proving that they no longer constituted a threat. Revolts against royal tax-collectors, sometimes embracing all social groups in a given locality, had been brutally suppressed. While similar protests flared up during the early years of Louis XIV's personal rule, they petered out in the 1670s.

Meanwhile the crown apparently had much less to fear from the constitutional opposition of representative bodies. The pretensions of the *parlements* had been resisted and defied. In July 1655 the seventeen-year-old king confidently rebuked the *Parlement de Paris:*

> Everyone knows how much your assemblies have incited troubles in my state, and how many dangerous effects they have produced. I have learnt that you presume to continue them again under the pretext of deliberating on my edicts which not long ago were read and published in my presence. I have come here expressly to forbid the continuation of your debate and to forbid you *M. le Premier Président* to allow or to agree to it.

During the Fronde there had been demands for the Estates General to settle the nation's problems and indeed in 1649 and in 1651 it was actually summoned. But it never met. As a result there was no equivalent to the English parliament which could claim to represent the whole nation. As for the provincial estates, they had been abolished in Provence, Normandy and Dauphiné and their powers reduced in Languedoc, Burgundy and Brittany.

Conciliar government at the centre had re-established a close working relationship with *intendants* in the localities, despite the Frondeurs' attempts to abolish them. Furthermore, the collection of taxes had been resumed not through the traditional channels of the *trésoriers* and *élus,* but once again through the more productive alliance of *intendants* and financiers. The provincial governors had decreasing opportunities to raise their provinces in revolt, not only because the *intendants'* eyes were upon them, but also because they had lost their monopoly of local patronage. Likewise the independence of the towns had been severely curtailed, as the crown had established its rights to control elections to municipal office and to influence urban financial income and expenditure.

However, it would be wrong to suppose that the king and his ministers could now exercise quasi-dictatorial powers. The crown's recovery from the Frondes was by no means as impressive as historians who read history backwards would have us believe. As far as contemporaries were concerned, the government's victory had been a close-run thing; there was still widespread awareness of living on the edge of a precipice. Furthermore, several factors continued to impose stringent limitations on the crown's coercive authority and freedom of manoeuvre. Slow communications, distance, and the passive disobedience of millions still stymied the effectiveness of central government. The provinces jealously guarded their local privileges which were guaranteed by laws which the crown could not overturn. While the nobles no longer resorted to armed revolt, they dominated the court which remained the source of power and patronage. The number of venal office-holders had now swollen to 60,000, a perpetual drain on the crown's financial resources and a guarantee of inefficiency. All attempts at retrenchment and reform came up against this huge morass of privilege and vested interest which not even the most self-confident and powerful Bourbon could afford to alienate. That had been Mazarin's mistake during his first five years of office - hence the Frondes. Furthermore, the absence of an institution similar to England's parliament representing the whole nation worked against royal power as well as in its favour, for the king could not easily mobilise national support by explaining his policies or appealing for help. In short, the question which was posed at the beginning of this book was if anything even more relevant in 1661 than in 1610: how was it possible for the government to ensure that it would actually be obeyed?

It is a particularly good question in 1661 because it is clear that in a very real sense the government was indeed being obeyed. It is not just a matter of Anne of Austria's successful defence of her son's authority and of Cardinal Mazarin's survival and personal enrichment, nor of the resilience of the *intendants* and financiers, nor of the defeat of popular revolts. The fact is that France was governed, even if one has to add 'after a fashion' and even if one has to agree that 'absolutism' on closer inspection means less and less. The most impressive proof of the government's relative effectiveness is the raising of money to finance the wars against the Habsburg powers. No revisionist historians can get around this indisputable achievement. However chaotic and hand-to-mouth the methods, a colossal amount of money was found so that the war could eventually be fought to a satisfactory conclusion. How was this done?

The answer to the question is clear. Bourbon 'absolutism' relied far less on naked force and far more on persuasion and the exploitation of men's greed and ambition than used to be appreciated. The name of the game was patronage. During Mazarin's tenure of office the system of clients, brokers and patrons which we noted in chapter 2 became increasingly influential and indeed decisive. Mazarin's inept handling of royal patronage due mainly to his own inexperience and ignorance of French politics was a major cause of the Frondes. Similarly the cardinal's quarrel with Condé arose partly out of a row about family marriages - which invariably involved patronage. But Mazarin learnt fast. The course and outcome of the aristocratic Fronde was decided as much by patronage as by force of arms. For instance the duc de Mercoeur, the son of Vendôme, one of Henri IV's bastards, became Mazarin's client and married Laura Mancini, Mazarin's niece, even though the cardinal was an exile in Cologne. Mercoeur's family strongly attacked him for marrying beneath himself. But Mercoeur was no fool. He guessed rightly that his father-in-law would come through the Fronde. When this eventually happened Mercoeur was unstoppable, eventually obtaining the governorship of Provence. During the dark days of the Fronde Mercoeur's support and loyalty to Mazarin and hence to the crown were highly valuable. The ability to assess which way the wind was blowing was indeed a prerequisite of success. For instance the influential cleric Daniel de Cosnac was grateful to his patron the prince de Conti who had procured for him the bishopric of Valence. But in autumn 1656 Cosnec deserted Conti whose star was clearly waning for Mazarin. Conti was furious, but Mazarin looked after his new client, making him first almoner in the household of the king's brother.

Force continued to play a key role, but it was most effective when combined with patronage. The recovery of royal control over Provence is an instructive story. Initially Mazarin had failed to perpetuate Richelieu's system of patronage which had kept this potentially unstable province reasonably loyal. But the combination of an unreliable governor (Alais) and factional in-fighting by the provincial *gros bonnets* (big wigs) plunged the province into chaos during the Fronde. Order was eventually restored by royal troops. But, as we have seen, Mazarin consolidated the government's position by appointing the duc de Mercoeur as governor and by recruiting local noblemen through the good offices of his broker, Henri d'Oppède. Mazarin rewarded d'Oppède handsomely and publicly indicated his favour by staying with him when the court visited Aix in January 1660.

Was this corrupt system which exploited people's vanity, ruthlessness and greed and which Sharon Kettering has called 'a blurred and bowdlerised form of feudalism' a source of strength or weakness to the crown? The answer was 'both', as had been clearly demonstrated during Mazarin's term of office. It could go disastrously wrong if ineptly directed. But if the controller of royal patronage knew what he was doing, it could make the crown supreme, not only in Paris or Versailles but in Brittany, Provence and other outlying areas. Louis XIV was to prove himself an adept manipulator of both men and gravy-trains. While thanks to his effortless charm and sublety he dominated his nobility at Versailles, he brilliantly exploited patronage in order to undermine the nobles' domination of the provinces. Thus political and social stability came to France. As in Hanoverian England, it was not a particularly edifying or inspiring stability, based as it was on interest and corruption. But it worked, and arguably it was better than anarchy.

However, while Louis XIV was able to exploit his social and political inheritance there were several features which militated against the true interests of most French people. We have noted the prevalence of these features during the years 1610 to 1661; now we have to recognise that by 1661 they had become accentuated. For instance the successful defence of privilege by aristocrats and office-holders had widened the gap between rich and poor. A similar process had occurred in the towns where the municipal oligarchs had exploited the opportunities of clientage at the expense of their less fortunate neighbours. In the villages too the gap had widened between wealthy peasants and the very poor. These injustices had been exacerbated by the system of tax-collection which offered ever-widening opportunities for self-enrichment to those who knew how to exploit the system.

Again, the escalating reverence for blue blood and for the aristocratic life-style had damaging implications for the French economy. Snobbery may seem relatively harmless or even just plain ridiculous, but in seventeenth-century France it had disastrous economic effects. The contempt for manufacturing industry, for methodical farming and for trade discouraged France's best minds from tackling her immense economic problems. The only respectable callings were the church and the army, the only socially acceptable life-style the pursuit of aristocratic correctness. This meant that money was invested in government bonds, the purchase of office or in land to be exploited as a status symbol rather than an economic investment to be nurtured and developed. In a similar way, the aristocratic acceptance of nationalist aggrandisement and of war as an instrument of policy dominated French decision-making. Both Richelieu and Mazarin clearly believed that prosperity at home came second to glory abroad. Louis XIV was their willing pupil. As a result, French trade, agriculture and industry were crippled so that expensive wars could be financed. In the meantime international and even French markets were cornered by the English and the Dutch. The point to stress is that this deplorable aristocratic bias was getting more and not less influential by 1661. As a result, French trade and industry were losing out to the Dutch and English to an increasing extent. In real terms French agriculture was increasingly inferior to English and Dutch rivals.

Did anyone dare to question this disastrously unbalanced scale of values? Seventeenth century French governments did not hesitate to persecute subversive thinkers. Richelieu reprimanded the youthful Paul Gondi as 'a troublesome spirit' and expelled from France Descartes, the greatest philosopher of the age. Pascal was likewise constantly in trouble as we shall see. Ideas were nevertheless circulating, intellectuals enjoyed some freedom of expression, and Paris enjoyed its gutter-press. Mazarin could not stop the *Mazarinades,* just as Louis XIV's policemen subsequently proved unable to prevent the circulation of scurrilous attacks on his public policies and private follies. Nor, as we shall see, could French governments from Richelieu to Louis XIV eradicate Jansenism. Given this relative freedom of expression, what had France to say? What was the state of public opinion when Louis XIV began to rule as well as reign? Had he anything to fear from subversive and radical criticism?

Not much, it would seem. The combination of Richelieu's propaganda and the memories of the Fronde had firmly established the French people's respect for monarchy. To a remarkable extent, French men and women forgave their rulers the horrors and deprivations of nearly half a century of war, the sufferings caused by fiscal terrorism and the warfare state, and the outrageously unjust and corrupt system of taxation. Instead of concluding that the system of unchecked monarchy was flawed, they put their faith in their new monarch. Louis XIII's cruelty, Richelieu's brutality and obsession with war, and Mazarin's slippery greed were all forgotten. Louis the Gift of God would prove to be God's gift to the nation. He would surely prove to be as handsome in deeds as he was in looks. True, the Fronde was a gift to monarchist writers and preachers. When one looked back to the chaos and bloodshed of the Fronde and to the selfishness and incompetence of the Frondeurs, how could one argue that there were viable alternatives to monarchy? It is significant that Molière, the most perceptive and successful critic of society in the early years of Louis XIV's personal rule, satirised religion, the medical profession, social-climbers - but never the monarchy. Indeed he crawled to Louis XIV.

If Molière is dismissed as an entertainer rather than a serious thinker, with what issues were France's real intellectuals concerned? The answer is that they were more preoccupied with the next world than with this world. While the case for absolute kingship seems to have gone through on the nod, rival claims to absolute theological truth were enthusiastically canvassed and contested. It tells us much about the priorities of the French educated elites during Mazarin's last years that the government's handling of theological problems caused more discussion than such bread and butter issues as taxation, economic policy and farming techniques.

The intellectual debate which excited educated French people in the 1650s and 1660s was the Jansenist controversy. Jansenism was a product of the French Catholic reformation - a dynamic and fruitful movement which inspired French Christianity during the first half of the seventeenth century, producing saints such as François de Sales and Vincent de Paul and intellectuals such as Cardinal Bérulle. Naturally this return to Christian basics led to demands for moral rigorism and high standards of personal living. The *dévots* responded positively to such challenges as did the Company of the Holy Sacrament (see page 23). In 1640, in pursuit of theological and moral excellence, Cornelius Jansen, bishop of Ypres in the Spanish Netherlands, published his *Augustinus,* a massive exposition of Saint Augustine's theories about predestination. Were people predestined before birth to eternal salvation or damnation as Augustine apparently taught, or was there an element of free will which affected mankind's eternal destiny as the Jesuits maintained? Paradoxically the Jansenists acquired a reputation for sanctity even though they believed that mankind's fate in the next world was fixed while the Jesuits were criticised for moral laxity even though they taught salvation by good works.

The conflict between Jansenist and Jesuits had certain political overtones. Throughout the seventeenth century the French kings' confessors were invariably Jesuits. Jansenists on the other hand were often in trouble with the authorities. We saw in chapter 3 how Jansen's friend Saint-Cyran infuriated Louis XIII by attacking the exploitation of reverence for the Virgin Mary in order to boost the French war effort. Richelieu locked him up as a dangerous subversive. Jansen bitterly criticised the French for fighting the Catholic Habsburgs. Both Cardinal de Retz and the duchesse de Longueville, who played a prominent part in the Fronde, patronised the Jansenists while we have noted Jansenist influences among the recalcitrant parish priests in Paris.

Unfortunately for the government, the Jansenists commanded considerable public support. These Catholic puritans' claims to personal sanctity were widely accepted so that their headquarters in Port Royal des Champs, a monastery near Paris, became a refuge for those who wished to renounce the world or recharge their spiritual batteries. The Jesuit claim that the Jansenists were heretics was hotly disputed. A prominent Jansenist Antoine Arnaud counter-attacked with his *De la Fréquente Communion* in which he criticised the Jesuits' facile and theologically unsound willingness to excuse sinners who attended a few communion services. The fact was that the church was in disarray over Jansenism in that to condemn Jansen was to condemn the highly respected and reputedly orthodox Augustine. When Mazarin persuaded an unwilling pope to issue a bull condemning Jansenism the *Parlement* of Paris refused to register it so that it finally had to be imposed by a l*it de justice*. The pope's actions provoked one of the most brilliant writers of the age Blaise Pascal to ridicule the Jesuits in his *Lettres Provinciales* - a publication which the government attempted in vain to suppress, though they persecuted its author.

In short Mazarin bequeathed an unsolved problem to Louis XIV which he had unnecessarily exacerbated. Very much his godfather's pupil and very much a child of his age, Louis shared his contemporaries' obsession with Jansenism which he was to handle with increasing ineptitude right up to the end of his long reign. The Jansenist controversy illustrates both the contrasts between seventeenth and twentieth century priorities and the very real practical limitations of what Bourbon 'absolutism' could actually achieve.

Nevertheless, Louis XIV had his triumphs. Indeed most of the problems which he inherited were tackled with impressive realism and flair. We have established that by no means everything was in his favour when he became his own chief minister. However, Louis appreciated that the secret of success was to convince the privileged and the rich that they had more to gain than to lose from co-operation with the crown. Despite the fact that it was not always easy to persuade them that this was so, Louis was on the whole remarkably successful, just as he was equally successful in imposing his own personality and scale of values on France and Europe.

Whether the triumph of Louis XIV's political and social influence was widely beneficial is debatable. We have seen that the half-century since Henri IV's death ended in France with the triumph of privilege and self-enrichment at the expense of those who could not defend their own interests. This trend was perpetuated by the Sun King. He himself was privilege and snobbery personified. He had no original ideas. Spiritually and intellectually Louis XIV was just the man to bring stability to the France which had been governed - and misgoverned - by the cardinals. In fact he was the cardinals' legacy to France. He was a good second-rater, deeply conservative, an opportunistic manipulator rather than a statesman, the uninspired creator of an uninspiring age. 'Where there is no vision the people perish' - as the Sun King's subjects were to discover.

Making notes on *'Conclusion: The Cardinals' Legacy to Louis XIV'*

The necessary material is provided in this chapter for you to assess the difference that the cardinals made to France. Of course not all the changes that occurred between 1610 and 1661 can be attributed to Richelieu and Mazarin. Nevertheless, they had great opportunities to change the face of France for good or ill. In particular you could with profit make careful notes on the political changes achieved. Update your notes on absolutism: in 1661 was France nearer or further from the absolutist state of the text-books? Make additions to your notes covering the question, 'Why was the monarchy obeyed?'. In general, was France now an early modern or still a late-medieval country? Especially if you are going to study Louis XIV's reign, you should adopt a purposeful approach to the Jansenist controversy. Make a careful note on the origins of the controversy, using the material in this chapter. Methodically summarise the legacy left by the cardinals to Louis XIV - the subject of the following essay.

***Answering essay questions on** 'Conclusion: The Cardinals' Legacy to Louis XIV'*

Consider the following question:

> Assess the weakness and the strength of the legacy of Richelieu and Mazarin to Louis XIV.

This is a question which you should be pleased to find in an exam paper, despite the facts that it is quite taxing and that it would be only too easy to make a mess of it. Avoid a narrative coverage of the cardinals' achievements and failures; such a treatment does not answer the question. And avoid assertions unsupported by facts ('Richelieu was the greatest servant France ever had'). Your objectives should be to establish what the legacy was, and then to assess its weakness and strength. The treatment must be analytical.

In your introduction stress the high reputations of Richelieu and Mazarin. Then emphasise the social and political instability inherited by Louis XIV. This is very much the conclusion of recent research; while there was much to play for, nevertheless Louis XIV was bequeathed great problems. What *was* the legacy for which the cardinals were truly responsible? What were its strengths and weaknesses?

Your development section first needs a paragraph in which you clearly establish what the legacy was. Then you should devote a paragraph to the strengths of that legacy - the defeat of the Fronde, the re-establishment of the *intendants,* the cultivation of pro-monarchy public opinion. Next you need a paragraph on weaknesses - financial problems, the office-holders, an unhappy, politically unstable country, problems of economic backwardness, social inequality and inefficient and unfair taxation wholly ignored.

Your conclusion is vital. You must assess - that is to say, evaluate. It does not matter whether you are generous or critical towards the cardinals, provided that you talk sense and answer the question.

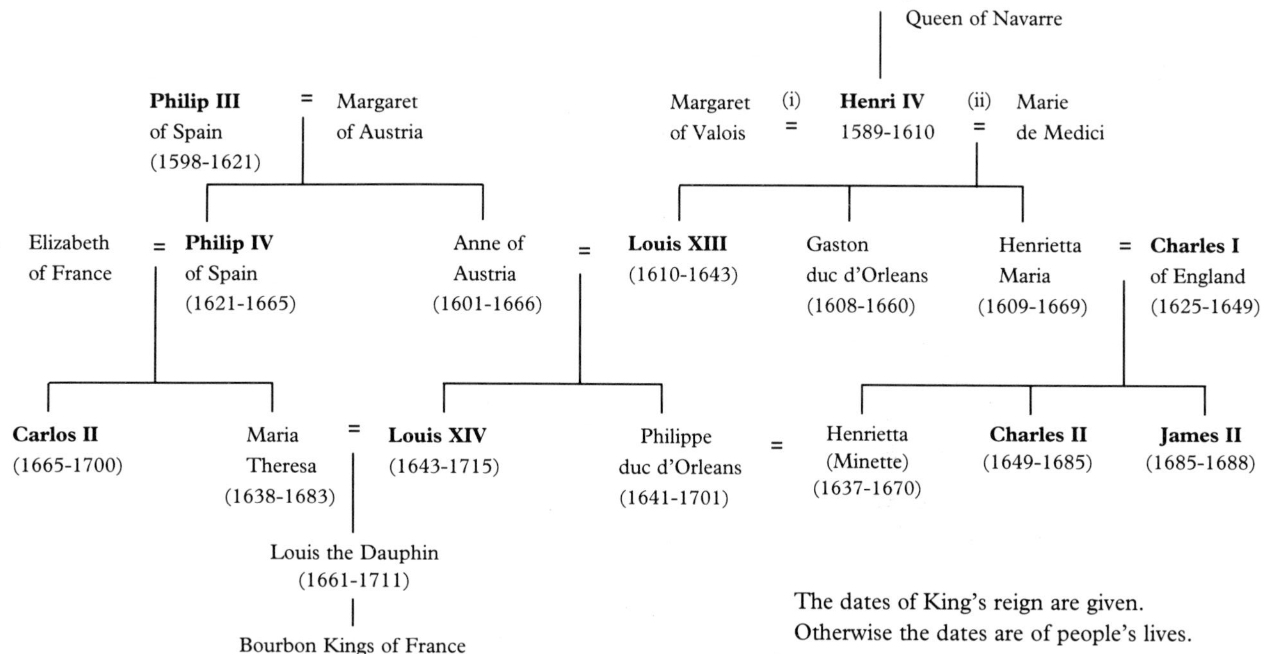

The Family of Louis XIII

Chronological Table

1610	May 14	Assassination of Henri IV. Louis XIII became king, Marie de Medici became regent
1614-15		Meeting of Estates General
1617	April	Louis XIII's coup. Murder of Concini
1620-1		War waged against the Huguenots. Death of Luynes
1622		Richelieu made a cardinal and admitted to the council
1624	August	Richelieu appointed chief minister
1626		Chalais conspiracy. Assembly of Notables
1627-8		War against England. Siege and capture of La Rochelle
1629		Peace of Alais with the Huguenots
1630		Capture of Pinerolo. Diet of Ratisbon
1630	Nov 11	The Day of Dupes
1631		Treaties of Barwalde with Sweden and Cherasco with Spain
1632		Suppression of Montmorency's revolt
1633		Vincent de Paul founded the Sisters of Charity
1635		France entered Thirty Years War
		Academie Française founded
1636		Spanish army reached Corbie. Performance of Corneille's *Le Cid*
1638	Sep 5	Birth of Louis XIV
1639		Revolt of the Nu-Pieds in Normandy
1640		Publication of Jansen's *Augustinus*
1642		Cinq-Mars conspiracy
	Dec 4	Death of Richelieu
1643	May 14	Death of Louis XIII. Accession of Louis XIV. Anne of Austria regent. Mazarin chief minister
	May 19	Battle of Rocroi (Condé defeated the Spaniards). Revolt of the *Importants*
1648	Aug 20	Battle of Lens (Condé defeated the Spaniards)
	Oct	Treaty of Westphalia ends the Thirty Years War
1648-9		*Fronde Parlementaire* (see detailed summary on page 118)
1650-3		The Fronde of the Nobles (see detailed summary on page 118)
1656		Publication of Pascal's *Lettres Provinciales*

1657-1658	Alliance with England. Battle of the Dunes
1659 Nov	Peace of the Pyrenees between France and Spain
1660 Jun	Marriage of Louis XIV and Maria Theresa
1661 Mar 9	Death of Mazarin

France and the Cardinals in context

1598-1621	Philip III king of Spain
1603-1625	James I king of England
1609-1610	Cleves-Julich crisis
1611-1632	Gustavus Adolphus king of Sweden
1612-1645	Michael Romanov Czar of Russia
1616	Death of Shakespeare
1618-1648	Thirty Years War
1619	Execution of Oldenbarneveldt
1619-1637	Ferdinand II Holy Roman Emperor
1621-1665	Philip IV king of Spain
1622-1642	Olivares chief minister in Spain
1625-1649	Charles I king of England
1628	Piet Hein captured Spanish treasure fleet
1631	Battle of Breitenfeld (Gustavus Adolphus beat the Spanish)
1632	Battle of Lutzen (death of Gustavus Adolphus)
1634	Battle of Nordlingen (Imperialist/Spanish victory)
1635	Peace of Prague necessitated French intervention
1637-1657	Ferdinand III Holy Roman Emperor
1640-1660	The Long Parliament met in England
1640	Revolts of Portugal and Catalonia against Spain
1640-1688	The Great Elector ruled Brandenburg
1642-1648	English Civil Wars
1649	Execution of Charles I. The Commonwealth in England
1652	First Anglo-Dutch war
1658	Death of Cromwell
1658-1705	Leopold I Holy Roman Emperor
1660-1685	Charles II king of England

Further Reading

a) Original Sources

Richard Bonney, *Society and Government under Richelieu and Mazarin* (Macmillan 1988).
J.H. Shennan, *Government and Society in France 1461-1661* (Allen and Unwin 1972)
Pierre Corneille, *Le Cid and Other Plays* (Penguin 1970)

b) Secondary works

Our understanding of the period has been transformed by recent scholarship. Some of the following books are quite demanding, but if you propose to study topics from this period in depth you cannot afford to ignore the works of historians such as **Richard Bonney, Orest Ranum** and **Sharon Kettering.** All these books should be obtainable from public libraries.

Richard Bonney, *Political Change in France under Richelieu and Mazarin* (Oxford 1978)
Richard Bonney, *The King's Debts* (Oxford 1981)
William Beik, *Absolutism and Society in Seventeenth Century France* (Cambridge 1985)
Sharon Kettering, *Patrons, Brokers and Clients in Seventeenth Century France* (Oxford 1986),
David Parker, *The Making of French Absolutism* (Arnold 1983)
Orest Ranum, *Richelieu and the Councillors of Louis XIII* (Oxford 1963)
Orest Ranum, *The Fronde - a French Revolution* (New York 1993)
Richard M. Golden, *The Godly Rebellion* (New York 1981)
S.A. Westrich, *The Ormée of Bordeaux* (John Hopkins 1972)
Robin Briggs, *Communities of Belief* (Oxford 1989)
R.R. Harding, *Anatomy of a Power Elite* (Yale 1978).
P.J. Coveney, *France in Crisis* (Macmillan 1977)
A. Lloyd Moote, *The Revolt of the Judges* (New York 1975)

c) The following biographies are interesting and well worth reading:

J.H. Elliott, *Richelieu and Olivares* (Cambridge 1984)
E.W. Marvick, *Louis XIII, the Making of a King* (Yale 1986)
J. Bergin, *Cardinal Richelieu. Power and the Pursuit of Wealth* (Yale 1985)

Robert Knecht, *Richelieu* (Longman 1991)
Ruth Kleinman, *Anne of Austria, Queen of France* (Ohio 1985)
G.R.R. Treasure, *Cardinal Richelieu and the Making of French Absolutism* (London 1972)
G.R.R. Treasure, *Mazarin* (Routledge 1995)
A.Lloyd Moote, *Louis XIII - the Just* (California 1989)
Georges Dethan, *The Young Mazarin* (Thames and Hudson 1977)
J.H.M. Salmon, *Cardinal de Retz* (London 1969)

d) In General

Victor-L Tapié, *France in the Reign of Louis XIII and Richelieu* (Cambridge 1984)
Robin Briggs, *Early Modern France 1560-1715* (Oxford 1977)
G.R.R. Treasure, *Seventeemth Century France* (Macmillan 1972)
David Maland, *Culture and Society in Seventeenth Century France* (Batsford 1970)
Robert Knecht, *The Fronde* (Historical Association 1971)
Orest Ranum, *Paris in the Age of Absolutism* (New York 1968)

All the books mentioned here have great merits. The general reader may well find the biographies most accessible, while the harassed examination candidate will be attracted by the brevity of **Knecht's** Historical Association pamphlet. **Briggs'** *Early Modern France* is an inexpensive paperback, full of stimulating ideas and is worth buying.

Index